Deliverance
"My Story, Your Victory"

By

Sherman J. Butler, Sr.

Copyright © 2011 by Sherman J. Butler, Sr.

Deliverance: *My Story, Your Victory*
by Sherman J. Butler, Sr.

Printed in the United States

ISBN 978-0-9831317-3-1

All rights reserved solely by the author. The author guarantees all contents are original and do not infringe upon the legal rights of any other person or work. No part of this book may be reproduced in any form without the permission of the author. The views expressed in this book are not necessarily those of the publisher.

Except where designated, all scriptural references are taken from the Authorized King James Version.

Cover and interior design by:
Latoya Bady
TBady Graphic Designs
Chicago Illinois
Tbady@live.com

Literary consultation services provided by: Dennis James Woods

Life To Legacy, LLC
P.O. Box 1239
Matteson, IL 60443
(877) 267-7477
Life2legacybooks@att.net

www.Life2legacy.com

Presented to:

To order this book go to:

www.PastorShermanJButlerSr.net

To email Pastor Butler:

butler9972@yahoo.com

Table of Contents

Dedication	i
Introduction	iii
Chapter 1 The Beginning of the Strongholds (The Early Years)	1
Chapter 2 College Years and Beyond	11
Chapter 3 The Road to Deliverance	14
The Brain Tumor	15
Chapter 4 At Your Weakest Point	18
Chapter 5 Communications Exile	27
Chapter 6 The Time Bomb Exploded!	32
Run For Your Life	36
Chapter 7 Stronghold Spirits	41
Anatomy of a Stronghold	44
Psychological Effects of Strongholds	50
Chapter 8 Demons	53
Soul-Ties	55
Ungodly Soul-Ties	58
Chapter 9 Receive Your Deliverance!	67
Seven Steps to Freedom	68
Chapter 10 Final Exhortations	83

Dedication

This book is most humbly dedicated to my lovely and loving wife, Rhonda Elaine Butler, who I've loved for more than twenty years of my life. She has been there with me and for me through thick and thin, for better and for worse. Rhonda, I thank you for every kind word and every critical word. Baby, you have listened to me even when I didn't always make a lot of sense. I thank you for going along with every crazy and wild idea. With your help, together we have a wonderful life. Thank you, baby.

I also dedicate this book to my late mother, Mother Jimmie Will Nalls-Butler. Mama, may your spirit rest in peace, because without you, I would not be where I am today. You were the first love of my life. Your prayers, love and encouragement were what kept me going. As long as I live, you will maintain a special place in my heart. You are in my thoughts every day.

I also dedicate this book to my children: Sherman, Jr., Sherrhonda, Sherrell, Shermiah, Byron, and LaTonya. Also to my father, Bishop Steven K. Butler, Sr.; my sisters Sylvia, Shelia (Alvin), Sandra (Brett); my brothers, Sammie, Salandra (Pamela), Steve, Jr. (Geraldine) and Sychem; my godchildren and their wives, husbands and children; and to my uncles, aunts, nephews, nieces and cousins.

I give a special dedication to my wonderful and inspiring godparents, Deacon William and Evangelist Alice Dice. Without your prayers, love and support, I could not have made it. This book is also dedicated to the great members of the church I pastor, Nazarene All Nations Church and all the Nazarene churches of Chicago and abroad; to every church and pastor who has allowed me to minister in their churches across the country and across denominational lines and doctrine; and to my many friends, thank you for your prayers and support.

 Finally, this book would be nothing if I could not thank the One who made it all possible, the One who gave and constantly gives me life, the One who created me in his image and in his likeness. He is Alpha and Omega, the Beginning and the Ending, the First and the Last. I love the Lord because He has forgiven me over and over again. God has healed my body, delivered my mind and soul, and freed my spirit. Thank you Lord God, for without you, nothing would be possible, and with you all things are possible. Without the Holy Spirit at the helm of my life to lead and guide me in all truth, I would have hopelessly tossed to and fro in the turbulent seas of life, like a ship without a sail.

Introduction

In the fourth chapter of the Gospel of Luke, we find two fascinating accounts in the life of Jesus that set the stage for his earthly ministry. The first event is the temptation of Christ, and the second event is his announcement of his earthly ministry in the synagogue at Nazareth. In Luke 4:1-13, we read about the temptation of Christ, which targets three strategic areas. In verses 1 and 2, we read about the first attack:

> ...And Jesus being full of the Holy Ghost returned from Jordan, and was led by the Spirit into the wilderness, being forty days tempted of the Devil. And in those days he did eat nothing: and when they were ended, he afterward hungered.

Here we find Jesus purposely being led by the Holy Spirit to be tempted by Satan. After Jesus had accomplished an extensive fast for forty days and forty nights, the scriptures tell us that He was hungry. Satan, seeing an opportunity to exploit this, came to Jesus to tempt him to use his miracle power for self-gratification by turning stones into bread. However, Jesus retorted by quoting from the scriptures. "And Jesus answered him, saying, It is written, That man shall not live by bread alone, but by every word of God." (Luke 4:4, where Jesus quotes Deuteronomy 8:3)

It is interesting that the first area the Devil attempts to

exploit is one of the strongest desires that human beings have: the desire for food and nourishment. Eating is a basic need for survival. When we are hungry, our bodies will make us aware of its need for nourishment with very strong cravings, which if left unsatisfied will eventually cause death. So here, we see the Devil's first tactic was to attack the weaknesses of the flesh.

The next temptation is found in verses 5-8, where the passage reads:

> And the Devil, taking him up into an high mountain, shewed unto him all the kingdoms of the world in a moment of time. And the Devil said unto him, All this power will I give thee, and the glory of them: for that is delivered unto me; and to whomsoever I will I give it. If thou therefore wilt worship me, all shall be thine. And Jesus answered and said unto him, Get thee behind me, Satan: for it is written, Thou shalt worship the Lord thy God, and him only shalt thou serve.

We have the Devil coming another way this time. In this temptation, he attempts to entice the Lord into submitting to him by showing him all the splendor of the kingdoms of the world. Satan hoped that after Christ saw all these things, the Lord's resolve to resist would be weakened. To sweeten the deal, the Devil said, "All this power will I give thee, and the glory of them." The Devil attempts to initiate the "lust of the eye," and mesmerize the Lord by showing the glory of all the world's kingdoms. How many times have people fallen into sin over things that they have seen and then coveted? Once again, Jesus' weapon is the Word of God, and He responds by simply saying in verse 8, "Get thee behind me, Satan: for it is written,

Thou shalt worship the Lord thy God, and him only shalt thou serve."

Not easily giving up, the Devil has one more wave of attack. Beginning in verse 9, the scriptures tell us:

> And he brought him to Jerusalem, and set him on a pinnacle of the temple, and said unto him, If thou be the Son of God, cast thyself down from hence: For it is written, He shall give his angels charge over thee, to keep thee: And in their hands they shall bear thee up, lest at any time thou dash thy foot against a stone.
>
> Luke 4:9-11

This time, the Devil attacks another area where men tend to have serious weaknesses, which is the "pride of life." The Devil uses the scriptures to tempt Christ, saying, "If you are really who you say you are, cast yourself down from here, because the scriptures say 'He shall give his angels charge over thee, to keep thee: and in their hands they shall bear thee up, lest at any time thou dash thy foot against a stone.'" The Devil was quoting Psalm 91:11 out of context. But, once again, Jesus resisted the Devil by also quoting scriptures and saying, "It is said, Thou shalt not tempt the Lord thy God" (Luke 4:12, where Jesus quotes Deuteronomy 6:16). After losing all three rounds, the bible says "when the Devil had ended all the temptation, he departed from him for a season."

In the passages that we have just examined, we see that there were three primary areas where the Devil tempted Jesus; the flesh, the eyes, and in pride. In 1 John, the Apostle warns us about these same areas when he writes:

> Love not the world, neither the things that are in the world. If any man love the world, the love of the Father is not in him. For all that is in the world, the lust of the flesh, and the lust of the eyes, and the pride of life, is not of the Father, but is of the world.
>
> 1 John 2:15-16

These are the same tactics the Devil used against Eve in the Garden of Eden. She "saw" (appealing to the lust of the eye) the fruit of the tree "was good for food" (appealing to the lust of the flesh) and by eating it, she and Adam would become wise and be like God (appealing to the pride of life). From all of this, we see that Satan's strategy to put us in bondage will always come in one of these three areas.

The next major theme of Luke chapter 4 comes after Jesus has been tempted. Passing the test, He was now ready to announce his ministry. When Jesus was led into the wilderness, verse 1 says He was *led* by the Spirit. But after He stood against the power of Satan and was victorious, the bible says that Jesus returned in the power of the Spirit. Now being in the power of the Spirit, He went to the synagogue in Nazareth, He opened the scriptures to Isaiah and quoted these powerful words:

> The Spirit of the Lord is upon me, because he hath anointed me to preach the gospel to the poor; he hath sent me to heal the brokenhearted, to preach deliverance to the captives, and recovering of sight to the blind, to set at liberty them

that are bruised, To preach the acceptable year of the Lord. And he closed the book, and he gave it again to the minister, and sat down. And the eyes of all them that were in the synagogue were fastened on him.

Luke 4:18-20

It is very interesting that after having won a crushing victory over the wiles and schemes of the Devil, Jesus announces his ministry founded upon "deliverance." He didn't start off by preaching wealth and prosperity, name it-claim it, and all of the other doctrinal fads that have been popularized today. But the Lord announces that one of the most important functions that He would fulfill would be that of Divine Deliverer. Since Christ is the Deliverer, this underscores a great spiritual truth: we all need deliverance in some shape, form or fashion.

As we can see from what we have covered so far, the topic of deliverance is a vast subject and is a major part of the Christian's walk with the Lord. It is a subject that is very close to my heart because what you don't know about deliverance can hurt you, or even kill you. That is why it is such a passion for me to communicate what I believe the Lord has given me to give to the Church. God has dealt with me to speak and teach deliverance. Like Jesus, I draw much passion and urgency when I read the prophet's words in Isaiah 61:1-3, the same words that Jesus read in the synagogue. I feel the fervency of Jeremiah when he said in Jeremiah 9:1, "Oh that my head were waters and mine eyes a fountain of tears that I might weep day and night for the slain of the daughter of my people."

Therefore, my mandate from God is to expose the devices and methods of Satan, how he seduces people to end up in bondage and do destructive things that can lead to damnation. No matter how the Devil dresses up iniquity, sin is not your friend. However, the only way for any of us to be freed from the clutches of the Devil is to have the proper weapons to wage war against him. Jesus is the Christ, the anointed one, the source of the anointing that has the power to destroy all yokes of bondage. Since He is the source of the anointing, He shares that anointing with us, so that we may remain free from all sorts of demonic entanglements.

As a pastor of a church, as a soldier in the army of the Lord, and as a servant of Jesus Christ, I too, have been anointed by God to preach deliverance to the captives, and recovering of sight to those who grope in spiritual blindness, and to bring a message of liberty to those who desire to be set free. The fact is, deliverance is a subject for everyone. The bible tells us that everyone needs to be delivered from something. No one is exempt. The scriptures clearly declare, "There is none righteous no not one," and "All have sinned and come short of the glory of God" (Romans 3:10 and 23). Therefore, we all have had something in our lives that we needed to be delivered from. David said, "Behold, I was shapened in iniquity; and in sin did my mother conceive me" (Psalms 51:5). From this passage, we understand that we were born into this world with a nature that is predisposed to sin. On our own, we have no power to change our sinful nature. However, this is exactly what the Lord came to deliver us from - sin and the penalty of sin. As the bible declares, the wages of sin is death, but the gift of God is eternal life through Christ Jesus our Lord (Romans 6:23).

Since Adam's original sin in the garden, we have been living in a fallen world. Therefore, many forms of wickedness that manifest upon humanity have been allowed by God as part of the curse for man's iniquity. There are demonic spirits that God permits to harass, oppress and in some cases possess people because of their constant disobedience to God's will. Once these spirits are attached, they cause conditions that modern medicine cannot cure and science and technology cannot explain. From this kind, only God's power can deliver you. Additionally, wickedness can bring multigenerational curses, as declared in Exodus 20:5, where God says, "visiting the iniquity (sin) of the fathers upon the children unto the third and fourth generation of them that hate me."

For example, homosexuality is a wicked sin that is against the natural order of intimate relations between a man and a woman. However, homosexuality is not only a sin, it's also a curse. If you get involved with someone who is manifesting a homosexual spirit, not only are you sinning with them, but their cursed lifestyle will be transferred to you. This is how a wide range of evil consequences come upon a person who practices this form of sexual wickedness.

Unfortunately, there are a lot of religious people who claim homosexuality is simply learned behavior, not inherited. They say this to reinforce the idea of tolerance. However, I beg to differ with them. Though all sins involve an act of the will, some actions and habits are demonically inspired and can transmigrate from one person to another, from one generation to the next. Here again is the essence of the cursed nature of homosexuality. This is why the bible admonishes us in Galatians, "Be not deceived, God is not mocked, whatsoever a man soweth, that shall he also reap…"

However, people can still be delivered from sins like homosexuality, as it says in 1 Corinthians 6:11, where the bible declares, "And such were some of you: but ye are washed, but ye are sanctified, but ye are justified in the name of the Lord Jesus, and by the Spirit of our God." Remember, there is nothing too hard for God, who is able to deliver you from anything that you truly want deliverance from.

When I prepared to write this book, I thought about all the people who need help and want to come out of bondage. However, many people don't know that they can come out of bondage, or even how to come out of bondage. As we seek answers to this dilemma, we must first understand that deliverance starts in the mind. The Bible says to "let this mind be in you, which was also in Christ Jesus" (Philippians 2:5). In order to be free, you have to let this mind be in you. You have to *permit* this mind to be in you. You have to want to be free. However, before you can want to be free, you have to know that you are in bondage. Many people don't know or believe that they are in bondage, because they are in agreement with the sins that have them bound.

Understand what Jesus said, "…Verily, verily, I say unto you, Whosoever committeth sin is the servant of sin" (John 8:34). All unrighteousness is sin. Sin is bondage, and all sin is of the Devil. You have to be hungry for deliverance. You have to want to be free. You have to tell yourself (and that spirit inside of you) this thing is not going to control me any longer! I refuse to be bound!

In 2 Timothy 1:7, the bible says, "For God hath not given us the spirit of fear; but of power, and of love, and of a sound mind." Courage and power come from the God that is within you. You must understand that each of us has God the light of God within us. Even though some people may appear to be too evil, it seems there can't be any God in them. But God's Light dwells in each of us. "In him was life; and the life was the light of men. *That* was the true Light, which lighteth every man that cometh into the world" (John 1:4,9).

One of the greatest stories told in the scriptures about the conflict between God and Satan is found in the book of Job. In the first chapter of Job, we find the basis for Job's troubles is an accusation Satan made against Job, saying that the only reason Job serves God is because God is good to him and has an impenetrable hedge of protection around him. To prove Satan wrong, God pulls down the hedge of protection and allows the Devil to get at Job. The point that is important to make here is that Satan cannot successfully attack a person who has God's hedge of protection around him.

I have been on both sides of the bondage issue. I know what it is like to be bound, and I know what it's like to be delivered. Therefore, I am strongly against the Devil and all of his strongholds because of the hold he once had on me. I emphasize "had" on me. While I was struggling with my stronghold, it had a very tight grip on me. I wanted desperately to be free. The reason I had so much difficulty getting free from this particular stronghold is because it's one of the strongest spirits in the Devil's arsenal. Many believe that this was the same spirit that was lurking in the Garden of Eden with Adam and Eve; that enticed Sampson to be with Delilah; that caused King David, "the apple of God's eye," to have Uriah killed; and that has caused many in the ministry to lose their anointing. This spirit and stronghold was the spirit of lust and illicit sex.

I wanted to write this book because of what that spirit did to me. Now I know that there are many strongholds and spirits, like alcohol, drugs, addiction to smoking, evil spirits, angry spirits, idolatry, witchcraft, depression, low self-esteem, homosexuality, and Satanism, just to name a few. Whatever the "it" is, they are all Satanically inspired, even though they may manifest themselves differently. Nevertheless, they are all wicked strongholds.

As a minister of the gospel, I have counseled many people with spirits, even extreme evil spirits. I have preached many messages and taught many bible classes on deliverance, always wanting to reveal the reason I felt I could help them. I always wanted to tell the people that I, too, had a stronghold on me that God delivered me from. I knew that if God could deliver me from sexual addiction, He could deliver them from anything. I also wanted to let people all over the world know that no matter how hard it may seem, they can be delivered.

I know many people who suffer with hidden addictions. Many people with addictions and strongholds try to hide them. Trying to hide something that is so much a part of you is very hard. I watched an episode of Oprah that featured men on the "down-low." These were men trying to hide their homosexuality. They tried to deny they were homosexuals by marrying women, having children and even going to church. They refused to admit that they had a problem. They sneaked out of their homes to have sexual intercourse with other men. They wanted to appear normal and not look bad to their families and friends. They tried to be someone they were not. As a result, the Devil ended up destroying their marriages through distrust, disease, and divorce. In short, the Devil will mess you up every time.

I also know many anointed and powerful men and women of God who have strongholds on them. They teach and preach, but they themselves need to be delivered. In Romans 11:29, we are told that the gifts and calling of God are without repentance. The word repentance here means without revocation. In other words, God gives gifts and callings that are not contingent upon our behavior or morality. God has given gifts to many people, but the gifts themselves are not validation of a true relationship with God. However, many believe that because they are gifted, they are in right relationship with God. This is where the enemy does some of his most diabolical deceptive work. A perfect example of this was Judas Iscariot, who was endowed with miraculous powers like the other disciples, but Jesus' testimony of him was that he was a Devil (see John 6:70).

Many people are anointed to preach and teach the gospel, and even to cause souls to be delivered, but they themselves will be disqualified. In 1 Corinthians 9:27, Paul gives us insight to how he maintained his deliverance, and the consequences of not doing so. The Apostle says, "I keep under my body, and bring it unto subjection: lest that by any means, when I have preached to others, I myself should be a castaway."

On Judgment Day, many who have been slaves to demonic strongholds will stand before the Lord pleading their case, saying, "Lord, Lord, have I not prophesied in thy name? And in thy name have cast out Devils? And in thy name done many wonderful works?" But Jesus says, "Then will I profess unto them, I never knew you: depart from me, ye that work iniquity" (Matthew 7:23). The fact that there will be many in that day implies that there is a serious problem in the church that will cause many to miss heaven because they are slaves to Satan, even though they think they are serving God. For these, I also wanted to write this book, and be the watchman on the wall to warn God's people.

I am sure you have heard many people say, "Just resist the Devil." However, resisting the Devil is an easy thing to say, but having the power to resist the Devil is another thing altogether.

The only thing that is effective in defeating the kingdom of darkness is the light of truth and the power of God. The bible says, "For the weapons of our warfare are not carnal, but mighty through God to the pulling down of strongholds" (2 Corinthians 10:4).

I have attempted many times to write this book. The Devil did not want this book to be written or published, because he does not want to be exposed. The Devil wants to continue to stay hidden so he can bring me back into bondage; and he certainly wants to exploit as many others as he can. In the beginning of this introduction, we covered the fact that before Jesus launched his ministry, He was first tempted by the Devil. However, after defeating the Devil, the scriptures inform us,

"And when the Devil had ended all the temptation, he departed from him for a season" (Luke 4:13). Here we learn an important spiritual truth. Even after you defeat the Devil today, it won't be long before he comes back to try again. I am not so foolish as to think that the Devil won't attempt to bring me back into bondage. He knows that since I'm a pastor, if he can get me to fall once again, many others will be affected, too. Satan, would love to ruin my testimony, so that after I have preached to others, I myself will become discredited and disqualified. Therefore, I know that he will return; but I will be standing ever ready to expose his unfruitful works of wickedness.

Chapter 1

The Beginning of the Stronghold
(The Early Years)

Before I begin to tell you my story, I feel that it is necessary to define the word stronghold. In biblical times, the term stronghold was well-known. However, back then it was more of a military term. Strongholds were typically encampments where an enemy of God's people, such as the Philistines, dug in and used that encampment as a base to coordinate and launch raids and attacks. In many cases, the stronghold was territory that was captured by the enemy and was now being used as a staging point to initiate and facilitate further attacks. Once the enemy captured a territory or city, they used everything in their arsenal to maintain control of that place. In other words, once they moved in, their intentions were to stay. And from that very place that they had taken, they continued to take more, so they could maintain, harass and control, until they had completely conquered their opposition.

When we speak of strongholds in the spiritual sense, these are areas of our lives that have been yielded to the enemy. He digs in and uses these areas to launch his attacks in order to bring and keep a person in bondage until he has completely destroyed that individual. Remember, the Devil's purpose is to kill, steal and to destroy. As a matter of fact, one of the Devil's names is Apollyon, which means the destroyer.

Strongholds typically come through the five senses, particularly through the eye gate, and will always be in one of these three areas: the lust of the eye, the lust of the flesh, or the pride of life. This is why in Galatians chapter five (verses 19-21), we get a partial list of the works of the flesh. However, once a person lets the enemy in by way of temptation, he seeks to exploit all the weaknesses of the flesh, which then leads to direct demonic influence.

In my life, the stronghold started with me at a very early age. I grew up in a very religious home, where my father was the pastor and my mother was the head mother of the church. When I was ten years old, I was sexually abused. I was inappropriately touched and fondled by an older, more experienced young woman. This was not my sin. It was not my fault. It was her sin and her fault, but nonetheless, that spirit transferred to me. This young woman would come over to our home and pretend to be playing with me, and all the while, she would be kissing me on my lips and touching me on my private parts.

At this age, I had never experienced anything like this

before. In my heart, I knew it was wrong, but physically I was aroused. Now I was left with a root of conflict and confusion. My young mind had been imprinted with this sensual memory, this tainted information that no ten year old should ever have to wrestle with. However, little did I know, I had been changed.

I was told never to say anything about this, and I didn't. I was left with all of the guilt, but attached to that guilt was the illicit desire for more sexual gratification, a desire that I would now have to grow up with.

Unknown to me at the time, the cloak of silence acted as a wedge between my mother and I. Even though we were very close, still I wouldn't tell her what was happening to me. All the while, the sexual abuse continued. Once this all started, this young woman would come over often. She too, was losing control. On several occasions, I tried to refuse her advances, but she would tell me that what she was doing was ok because she loved me, and that I was very special to her. So now, the enemy was carefully building a foundation of sexual perversion because he used her actions to connect illicit sexual gratification with love. Each time I would feel bad about what I was partaking in, I would be soothed with the words, "I love you. You are special." So even though I felt guilty at this point, I wouldn't stop her. Now I was given over, and not only was I interested in sex, I wanted more. This is a very important point. Satan wants to corrupt us when we are young and impressionable so he can have his way with us for life. So now this young woman's sin became mine. The spirit that was on her transferred over to me. As I look back at it, this same young woman at one time was an innocent child, just like me, until one unsuspecting day, someone that she probably knew and trusted, crept into her room and stole her innocence, the same way she stole mine.

Not too long after I had been sexualized, my interest in sex grew. I would start touching and feeling on girls. I would sneak and rub my private parts against girls' bodies. That incidental brush up against them, or that accidental touch near their private parts, were all part of my way of satisfying my growing lust.

As my interest in sex continued to grow, I started looking at various department store catalogs, fantasying about the women I saw in their underwear. Soon I had many catalogs in my bedroom. When my mother would see them and ask why I had all these catalogs in my room, I would lie and say that I was looking at shoes or something else. Soon, pictures of women in their lingerie was not enough to satisfy my growing lust. I graduated from catalogs to pornographic magazines. Since you could not get these magazines for free, I earned money emptying the neighbor's garbage so I could buy pornography. After buying these magazines, I would bring them home and stay up late at night to look at them – it was exciting and arousing.

Soon, still photos of nude women were not enough. I progressed to watching sexually explicit movies that aired on cable television. Our family didn't have cable. However, back then, cable television wasn't as advanced as it is now. Back then, all the shows came over on the same signal. You only needed a scrambler to see certain stations. If you got your hands on a scrambler, you could get adult programming without paying. Someone in our neighborhood had a scrambler that allowed us to see these cable programs, however, these scramblers weren't always perfect.

Most of the time, the adult shows would come in very snowy and have a thick line in the middle, and you could not see clearly what was going on. But the audio portion came in clearly and you could hear the action. In order to watch these shows you would have to turn your head a certain way. It was very tricky, but if you turned your head to the side, you could see one part of the action above the line and the other part of the action under the line. Needless to say, I had many neck cramps in the morning. I mentioned this because in all this seemingly harmless, so-called fun, it further demonstrates how the enemy gets you in progressively deeper. Like a drug addiction, sexual promiscuity can have so much control that you are willing to go to any length to get gratification.

The stimulation that I was receiving through my eye gate was not enough. I remember one late night while watching ON TV, I started soothing my privates and it felt really good, and before I knew it, I was stimulated. At this point, I didn't know what was happening, but it was very stimulating. The first night, I stopped stimulating myself before anything happened. At first I didn't know what would happen, but I wanted to find out. Each night I would sooth myself until it felt real good. Many mornings I would wake up sore. I started to mention this to my mother, but I said nothing. Still being torn between the guilty feelings and the erotic arousal, I stopped experimenting for a while. However, the desire to pleasure myself was too strong and I started pleasuring myself frequently.

I found myself doing it in the morning, afternoon, anytime and always. I would sometimes make up an excuse to go to the bathroom during school just to satisfy the growing lust within me. Soon, I was habitually seeking to gratify myself in this manner. Once again, the enemy introduced me to a behavior that I could not control. Now I understand that frequent pleasuring one's self is inspired by a demonic spirit.

Unfortunately, I have heard people say that it is natural and everybody does it. Well maybe everybody is not doing it. I understand that human sexuality is normal. And I also understand that particularly when we reach puberty, the changes in our body as we mature bring some discovery and curiosity. But this cannot be used as an excuse to give the Devil a way in to exploit our natural interest in the opposite sex. Additionally, my sexual expression was not the result of a wet-dream, where ejaculation occurs naturally while dreaming. My sexual involvement came as a result of being molested by a woman who was obviously manifesting a spirit of lust of her own.

Masturbation can be inspired by demonic forces and will lead you to doing other things. That's because masturbation will allow you to experience a level of sexual gratification, but it will never be completely fulfilling. Since it must be accompanied with a sexual fantasy, soon the individual will want to experience the reality, not just the fantasy. Once these fantasies are imbedded in your mind, the stronghold is set, and from that basis, you launch out to fulfill your lust in person-to-person ways. Therefore, this so-called innocent masturbation can lead you to molestation, fornication, rape, homosexuality and many other evil sexual spirits.

This is what happened to me. I wasn't satisfied with just pleasuring myself. I wanted to have sex with a girl. Many times, I would find a girl to pleasure me or give me a hand job. This erotic behavior brought me great satisfaction. I would then begin to stimulate her as well. This continued until one day while we were "doing" each other she pulled me inside of her. This was my first sexual intercourse experience.

This is what I meant when I said you can't just do a little something. This is why the bible warns us to flee fornication, because once you take that sexual leap, you cannot stop yourself from falling (1 Corinthians 6:18). The Devil's purpose is to always take you deeper and deeper into this pit of sin, until you are in over your head, where you cannot get out.

Once I had my first experience with sexual intercourse, I couldn't just kiss and touch, I always wanted to go all the way. Unfortunately, there are many young girls and young women who are willing to go all the way. They may look young and innocent, but they are giving themselves over to this spirit of sex. Sex is too powerful a spirit for parents to avoid talking to their young children about. The worst thing that a parent can do is stick his or her head in the sand, and not deal with talking to the children about sex.

The "sex talk" your parents are supposed to have with you never happened with me. My father seemed too afraid to talk to me about anything one-on-one. So he would say things over the pulpit like, "Children, stop doing things you have no business doing." We all knew what he was talking about, but that never stopped us. I wish he would have taken the time to

Deliverance

talk to me about "the birds and the bees," but he never did. Now that I am a parent, I find that sex is a hard subject for most parents to talk about, so I don't put the blame for what I did on my father.

I see many religious families unable to communicate with their children about most subjects one-on-one. They try to tell their children in other ways. Parents need to develop a relationship with their children so that the children will feel comfortable talking to them. Yes, this is easier said than done! I have also found that it doesn't matter how close you are with a parent, it is still hard for the child to tell his parents what he is going through. Most young people are afraid to talk to their parents about personal things like sex. Even in my case, I was very close to my mother, and I was still unable to talk to her about my feelings about sex, or why I spent so much time in the bathroom. The closest my mother and I have come to talking about sex was when she would admonish me by saying, "Boy, I don't want you to be bringing no children in here until you are married." One day she actually asked me if I was doing anything with this particular girl that she didn't like. I knew she was talking about sex and I told her, "No, mama." She then would quote Revelations 21:8, "all liars will have their part in the lake that burns with fire and brimstone." Those words have always stayed with me, but they didn't change my behavior; threatening people with hell rarely does.

Parents, it is important that you talk to your child about sex and any other subject that they may be dealing with. The child may not want to hear it, but you must continue to talk to them, pray for them and pray with them. As the bible says in

Proverbs, train up a child in the way he should go, and when he is old, he will not depart from it. This doesn't mean that the child will not make mistakes. It means the truth will not depart from him, and eventually, with love and support, he will find a way to do what is right.

I remember many days rubbing a girl's feet in the back of the church. Rubbing a woman's feet can be very sensual. It was great satisfaction for me. After church and between services, we would go to the store or take a walk around the church and commit many sexual acts. There were many "innocent" sexual acts going on around the church on many occasions.

Throughout my life, I have done many inappropriate sexual things that are very shameful. As I have already disclosed, this spirit of illicit sex continued to dog my steps for years. All these promiscuous behaviors started at an early age and the inclination to act out sexually increased as I grew older. Demonic spirits will always try to drag you deeper into the cesspool of debauchery and sin, so they work on your weakness. I liked the way a female felt. And my flesh enjoyed being a so-called slick and cunning hunter. I didn't discriminate between women. I would talk to all girls and young ladies. I was under the delusion that all women loved me, because through my convoluted mind, I thought that these women wanted to have sex with me. Whereas most of us have a preference in who we might consider for intimate relations, I had none. I liked all women, no matter whether they were fat, skinny, of a dark or light complexion, tall, short, or even crazy. Even blind girls and girls considered ugly by others were attractive to me.

Once I entered high school, this stronghold spirit began

to get out of control. I remember many days being in the back of the band room, where I was supposed to be practicing. I was practicing alright, but it wasn't with a musical instrument. I also remember going to band camp. I would sneak into the rooms of the girls and do all kinds of things. The band matrons or chaperones never caught me. Proms and other events were simply openings for me to express my sexual spirit. Today as I look back at it, my spirit shutters just to think of the things that I was doing. Thank God for his grace and mercy, that I never ended up in serious trouble. Soon I had to come to grips with the fact that this problem does not simply go away; you have to get help, the help of the Lord Almighty, and someone who is skilled to confront the subtlety of sexual strongholds.

Chapter 2

College Years and Beyond

After high school, I attended the University of Illinois at Chicago (UIC). Going to college and having a stronghold spirit of sex on me was like a child going to the candy store. I was around all kinds of women, big, fat, tall, skinny, and women of different nationalities. Wow! I was now talking to Hispanic, Asian, Indian, African, Jamaican and White girls.

Do you know when this spirit is on you, you don't need to approach them? They will approach you. That is because spirits carry a charisma that attracts people who are also manifesting or open to that spirit. I had girls coming up to me and talking to me. Every girlfriend I had, I cheated on her. I couldn't stay with a girl more than three months before I would cheat on her.

When I got involved with my last girlfriend, this spirit

was still on me. We broke up many times because she was not having it! She always suspected that something was going on behind her back. Sometimes her intuitions were right.

However, this particular young lady was different than all the rest. The true love that I had been longing for – a longing which had been suppressed because of my condition - I found in her. At that point, I realized that I really was in love with her. This became evident to me after she got tired of my games and left me. When this happened, it broke my heart and I broke down and cried. Now I was really angry with this sprit that had been causing me these problems all these years. Up until this point, I was in agreement with this spirit. We were buddies. It got what it wanted, and I was getting what I wanted, so there was an unspoken mutual agreement between us. However, when this spirit sought to destroy the only true relationship that I ever had, I was deeply disturbed.

This young lady was a true Christian, and was serious about her walk with the Lord. She stood up to me, and insisted that she wasn't going to have sex with me until we got married. I agreed with this until I couldn't take it any longer. So being driven by lustful passion, I asked her to marry me. Before we were engaged, I really started working on her resolve to remain celibate until marriage. So I tried a softer method of persuasion saying that sex was ok because we were already practically married anyway. This is a tactic that guys use in the church all the time. Once we were actually engaged, I began to pressure her more and more for sex. I remember saying anything and everything to get her to give in. And finally she succumbed to my desires and we had sex. We both knew it was wrong, and we sat up in church every service as if nothing had ever happened, even though we were committing fornication all throughout the week.

Chapter 3

The Road to Deliverance

Living in sin and being a hypocrite was beginning to take its toll on me. Many times, guilt would overwhelm me and I would become full of anxiety and depression. This was because I would get so high pursuing and having sex, but often the associated guilt and shame for being out of the will of God caused me to fall to great emotional lows. However, one day something happened that changed everything. I experienced a severe headache. Though it was painful, I considered it to be an isolated incident and I didn't attach any real concern to it. I remember taking some Tylenol and expecting the headache to go away – but it didn't.

When the next morning arrived, I went to work as usual and I told my supervisor about my severe headaches. Being concerned, they gave me some more medicine, but the pain continued, so they had to rush me to the hospital. They examined me there at the emergency room, but didn't detect anything, so they gave me some more medication and sent me home. The next day, the pain returned, but it was so excruciating that I was unable to go to work. I called in sick and asked my fiancée Rhonda to accompany me to the hospital.

All this time, I thought maybe my headaches were being caused because I needed glasses or something, because when I had the headaches I could not see clearly out of my left eye. However, I was wrong. It was something a lot more serious than an ocular headache. The doctors gave me an x-ray and made me wait in the waiting room. I waited for almost two hours. I asked the receptionist if they were finished with me and she said she believed they were. Before we made it to the elevator, the doctor came looking for me. He brought me back into the room and began to talk to me about what the x-ray turned up. He said he found an abnormality on the x-ray and that I needed to be admitted into the hospital for more observation. That scared me, so I called my mother and she rushed to hospital. After she arrived, I was admitted.

The Brain Tumor

Still not sure what was causing the headaches, we anxiously waited for the doctor to come and brief us. That's when he informed us that they found the cause of my headaches. The x-ray found a walnut-sized brain tumor blocking my optic nerve. So my doctor ordered me to undergo a battery of tests to determine whether the tumor was malignant (cancerous) or benign (noncancerous). Either way, I still would have to undergo neurosurgery to remove the tumor.

However, after laying up in the hospital waiting to have this surgical procedure done, this stronghold spirit of sex continued to oppress me. But now it seemed stronger than ever.

The Devil began his diabolical persuasion saying, "If this is the end, you might as well enjoy it." So I used this to gain sympathy from my fiancée. I persuaded her to have sex with me right there in the bed in my hospital room, even though I was getting visitors, let alone hospital staff, who could have walked in at any time. However, the Devil doesn't care. He wants to use, exploit, embarrass and make a fool out of you. Still, I allowed that spirit to take over me!

One day I received a phone call that changed the course of my life. I'll never forget it. The call was from an evangelist at our church named Evangelist Mattie L. Springfield. Evangelist Springfield was unable to come to the hospital due to an illness that she was struggling with at that time. After I answered the phone, she said these inspired words. "God knows all about you. He understands who you are and what you're going through in your life. Stop what you're doing. Make a change in your life. Get saved and get about God's business. Make a commitment to God and He will heal your body. God has a great calling on your life." My God. I was dumbfounded. Her words, oh, her words. They spoke to my heart. Her words spoke directly to my condition. Her words spoke to the pain that I had been carrying since the day my childhood was stolen from me! Her words, God's words, comforted my weary soul, comforted my physical pain, and even that dreadful spiritual pain. He spoke to me the words of life, the words of healing, the words of deliverance. This conversation has lived with me and will live with me forever as a memorial of God's great love for me.

I knew after this that I had to confess my sins and ask God for forgiveness and deliverance from all my sins. I knew at that moment I had this tumor because of the sexual stronghold, and God wanted me to stop. He wanted me to speak to the young and old, and tell them they can be delivered from whatever spirit that's controlling them. So God fulfilled his word of prophecy that He spoke through Evangelist Springfield. Indeed, I was totally healed of the brain tumor through the fervent effectual prayers of the righteous, my parents and all the saints who were praying for me.

The reason I say that I was totally healed from that tumor is because that tumor did not just represent a physical malady, but it represented a tumor that was placed in my soul the day that woman violated me. The same day my youthful innocence was stolen from me. That old ugly tumor that caused me so much pain and kept me from seeing God clearly, is now gone. Yes, that old ugly tumor was destroyed by He who hung on an old rugged cross, my Savior and Deliverer forever, Jesus Christ.

Chapter 4

At Your Weakest Point
(The Passing of My Mother)

    In the introduction, we covered the temptation of Christ. From our study of that event, we learned some of the tactics of the Devil as it pertains to the exploitation of areas of human weaknesses. We saw that after the Lord had fasted for forty days, the Devil came to him tempting him to turn stones into bread to satisfy his hunger. The Devil knew that the fact that Jesus was practically starving would be the perfect inroad for him to get the Lord to submit to the Devil's evil dictates. From this we must learn that the Devil is always looking for a weakness that he can exploit. The Devil does not fight fair. He is a dirty fighter. He'll kick you when you are down. He'll stomp on your fingers when you are barely hanging on because his purpose is to destroy you.

After having to struggle with all of my issues, I also had to walk through the valley of the shadow of death, when my sainted mother went home to be with the Lord. The passing of my mother was extremely difficult for me. Yes, I was a grown man, saved and sanctified, a minister of the Gospel and married with four children – yet despite of all that, I had a difficult time adjusting to life without my mother. I loved my mother very dearly. I would do anything for her. We were very close. She was always there whenever I needed her. On many occasions, it was my mother who prayed for me whenever I would be going through. It was my mother who would touch and agree with me in prayer whenever I was believing God for a breakthrough. It was my mother who was full of wisdom and whose godly counsel I could trust. During my hardest test in the church, it was my mother who encouraged me: "Hold on son! Things will get better after awhile. Stay in the church and stay with God." Truly, she was my inspiration.

As you could imagine, after she passed, I became very depressed. In fact, I became so depressed that I didn't see a reason to stay with God. Like a lot of people who have lost loved ones, I blamed God for taking her away from me. "God, you say that you are all powerful. You say that you'll never leave us or forsake us. You say that you love us, so why did you take my mother, the first person that believed in me, and the person I could tell my problems to. This was my indictment against God. And this was the reason that I never wanted to serve a God who would take someone who always prayed, fasted and believed in him. Certainly, now there was a gaping hole in my heart, a hole that turned out to be an open door for that ugly serpent to slither his way back into my life.

During the time my mother made her transition, I was attending Devry University. However, there was a spirit of despair that had taken hold of me. I was like a zombie, extremely depressed, merely existing, just going through the motions, like I had nothing to go on living for. It was very difficult for my children to see their father in that condition, the one they looked up too. This was also difficult for my wife, who would often try to encourage me by saying, "You still have us. I'm here for you. The children are here for you, too." But, there was nothing my wife or family could do to bring me out of this. I didn't feel like talking to anyone about how I was feeling, so I retreated into a shell, an emotional prison of my own making.

This is right where the Devil wanted me to be, emotionally withdrawn and socially isolated. The Devil doesn't want you to have any hope when you are going through your test and trials. He wants to keep you in depression, emotional oppression, and a constant state of unbelief, so he has the tools to dig you in deeper. Satan knows that once you are cut off from your support systems, he can have his way with you. He wants you alone. He wants you depressed. He wants you angry with the world, and particularly angry with God.

Once the Devil shipwrecks you all alone on pity-party island, the only company he will send you will be other evil spirits that will entice you to engage in anything that is a weakness in your flesh. They will tell you to eat, drink, do drugs, and have sex, anything that is your stronghold. Yes, the Devil prescribes a dose of sin to make the pain go away. No one likes pain. But unfortunately, we have bought into the concept called the pleasure principle, where the alleviation of pain is the most important thing to maintain and to achieve. But pain is important. That's the way we know something is wrong that needs our attention. However, it is the way you relieve your pain that makes all the difference in the world. When we are in pain, that is the time when we are also the weakest. And the Devil works on your weaknesses! This is why the Lord rejected Esau, who traded his birthright for a bowl of soup (Hebrews 12:16). This is also why the bible says to have no confidence in the flesh (Philippians 3:3), and why Jesus said the spirit is willing, but the flesh is weak (Mark 14:38).

In 2 Corinthians 10:4, we are instructed that "the weapons of our warfare are not carnal, but mighty through God to the pulling down of strong holds...." In this passage, we find some very important spiritual truths that are of great importance in relationship to the subject of deliverance. The first word is "weapons," which is connected to the second important term in this passage, "warfare." First of all, we must understand that when we were saved, we entered a battlefield where there was an ongoing war being fought between the Kingdom of Light and the Kingdom of Darkness. Christians are citizens and soldiers of the Kingdom of Light. All of the unredeemed and the Devil and his angels comprise the Kingdom of Darkness. Those of us who are in the army of the Lord must learn how to effectively fight the enemy, just as a person who has enlisted in the Marine Corp. However, as the passage tells us, our weapons are not carnal, or of this world. You cannot fight against demonic principalities and powers with an M-16. We need the proper weapons, the right tactics and effective armor in order to defeat the Devil's strongholds. All of this is the essence of what is called "Spiritual Warfare," the ability to effectively fight against and defeat the enemy.

When I look back to the sexual abuse that was perpetrated upon me at the age of ten, for a long time I only blamed the woman who committed these heinous acts. However, she was not the only person involved, because there was a demonic force behind her actions. This doesn't relieve her of any culpability; she still must give an account before the Lord. However, there are demonic principalities and powers lurking in the unseen realms that inspire such wickedness. Look at what the scriptures tells us in Ephesians 6:

> Finally, my brethren, be strong in the Lord, and in the power of his might. Put on the whole armour of God, that ye may be able to stand against the wiles of the Devil. For we wrestle not against flesh and blood, but against principalities, against powers, against the rulers of the darkness of this world, against spiritual wickedness in high *places.*
>
> Ephesians 6:10-12

In this passage, the Apostle Paul informs us that we are not fighting against mere human beings, but behind the people are real demons in the unseen realms. In the above passage, demons are referred to as *principalities, powers, rulers of the darkness, spiritual wickedness.* These are the spiritual culprits behind the wickedness perpetrated by people. Then in verses 13-17:

Wherefore take unto you the whole armour of

> God, that ye may be able to withstand in the evil day, and having done all, to stand. Stand therefore, having your loins girt about with truth, and having on the breastplate of righteousness; And your feet shod with the preparation of the gospel of peace; Above all, taking the shield of faith, wherewith ye shall be able to quench all the fiery darts of the wicked. And take the helmet of salvation, and the sword of the Spirit, which is the word of God:

As soldiers in the army of the Lord, we must know the tactics of our enemy and have the right armor and weapons to fight back. One of our primary offensive and defensive weapons is the Sword of the Spirit, which is the Word of God. This is exactly what Jesus used when He was being tempted by the Devil. He didn't argue, debate or try reasoning with the Devil. He didn't give the Devil his opinion, tell the Devil how foul a spirit he was, or anything like that. What Jesus did was stand on the Word of God each time. As the bible says in Hebrews 4:12, "For the word of God is quick, and powerful, and sharper than any two edged sword, piercing even to the dividing asunder of soul and spirit and of the joints and marrow." If we fight in the flesh, the Devil will defeat us every time, but there is nothing He can do with the Word of God.

Unfortunately, while I was in this funk, no scriptures seemed to come to me. Fighting spiritual warfare wasn't on my mind. And besides that, no matter what people said, it didn't matter. Therefore, the Devil exploited my depression and enticed me to deal with my pain by acting out sexually. While in this funk, I met several women. These women were young, very attractive and full of life. The enemy made it seem like all of them wanted to talk to me and be around me. These women would seem to have special interest in me and would buy me food and gifts. However, I would give the gifts away or back to them.

One day, one of these women's car broke down. She was very friendly and I could see myself getting weak around her. However, I continued to pray and hold onto my relationship with God and to my wife and family. During this time, my wife didn't seem to understand what I was going through. She seemed distant and cold. She wasn't very talkative, but that's her typical personality. Little did she know at this time that I needed her to be closer to me than ever before – but I wasn't helping the situation. So I began to find comfort in this other young lady.

It was during this same time that her car broke down and she asked if I would take her to work, pick her up from work, take her to school and back to her home. I should have seen this as a setup, but I justified it by thinking this was all in the normal process of me going to work and school. I began taking her to work, school and back home every day for about a week. During our rides, we had many conversations. On the days where my spirit was down, she noticed my unhappiness. In an attempt to show concern, she would ask if there was anything wrong. Though I would deny it, I could not hide the obvious. She saw through my thin veil of denial and intuitively knew something was wrong. She seemed so concerned and would always find something to say to cheer me up. On occasion, she would ask if I wanted to stop for something to eat. The Devil was really starting to work because "the fastest way to a man's heart is through his stomach." Whenever I said no, she would bring some food with her. Then at the end of the week, she asked me how much she owed me. I told her she didn't owe me anything.

On the last day of these rides, she wanted to ride in the back of my van. I asked her why she wanted to ride in the back. She said that she was tired and just wanted to stretch out. So she laid in the back as if she was going to take a nap. Then she asked me to pull over to a parking lot. I asked her why. She said just pull over. When I looked back, I could see she was completely naked. I asked what she was doing. She said she wanted to thank me and make me feel better. I pulled over and got out of the van, and the Devil began to tell me that I could get away with it. "No one would ever know."

Then the Devil came another way. He said, "God will forgive you." He told me that I deserved this because my wife wasn't being attentive to my needs. In an instant, all of these thoughts went through my head. Each one of them sounded good. I started to give in to this intense temptation and I started to walk around to the back side-door. I touched the door handle and suddenly I saw a vision of my mother, and my beautiful wife, and a cross. After seeing this, I gained the strength to resist the Devil. I couldn't go through with it. Thank God! I went back around to the driver's seat, started the van and drove her home. I explained to her that I couldn't go through with it because I had something stronger inside me. I explained to her that no matter what feelings I was feeling and how depressed and frustrated I was, I had something inside me that was greater than the desire for sex. It was at that defining moment that the truth of 1 John 4:4 came to life: "Ye are of God, little children, and have overcome them: because greater is he that is in you, than he that is in the world."

At that point, I suddenly realized how deep a pit of depression and despair I was in. All those years, I had been locked up in my mind and heart, imprisoned by acts perpetrated on me when I was only a child. Being tormented by my past, and devastated by the passing of my sainted mother, I finally reached the end of a road that I had traveled for far too long. It's strange how bad things can turn out for our good. At times, I thought I was gone too far for anyone to help me. But God, who is rich in mercy, saved me and pulled me up out of that horrible pit.

I realized that no matter how much you are depressed and down - you may be going through a death, loss of finance, a divorce, separation or whatever it may be - you cannot forget to stay in constant prayer and connection with the Lord and those who you love. "And he spake a parable unto this end, that men ought always to pray and not to faint" (Luke 18:1).

In Luke 4, after Jesus was tested, He returned in the power of the Spirit. Now that I have made it through my test, I also have returned in the power of the Spirit. You need the Holy Ghost. In Acts 1:8 the bible says, "But ye shall receive power after that the Holy Ghost is come upon you." Your deliverance is not complete until you receive the power of the Holy Ghost – that's the only way you can stand firm.

Chapter 5

Communications Exile

Despite the sexual abuse that I experienced as a young child, I have always been a very friendly and outgoing person. I have always had one of those engaging personalities that loves to meet new people and strike up a conversation. Typically, once people start talking with me, it's just like they have known me for years. This has been a good thing on one hand, but a bad thing on the other hand.

Years after my mother died, I was in a constant state of depression. And I was still wrestling with the skeletons from my past – things that I had not yet been delivered from. As I look back at it, I can see how I was being set up by the enemy. I began to think about my mother all the time. I wasn't earning the same level of income to which I had grown accustomed, and my employer was not open to giving me a raise. On the home front, my wife and I stopped communicating, while at the same time, there were several women outside my marriage to whom I grew closer. Many of these women were fellow students at Devry University. However, even in meeting these new acquaintances, there still seemed to be some obvious inconsistencies going on with me. They could not understand what was wrong.

At first when we met, I was always the "happy" one. Nothing seemed to depress me or get me down. I was always the encourager and was full of good advice. I was the one they came to when they were having problems. These women had many relationship problems in their lives, like difficulties with their boyfriends, husbands, or even difficulties finding a man. I was always the one they could come and talk to. I was the good listener who seemed to understand. But little did I know at the time, I was treading on thin ice, because none of these women were saved or even attended church, and I was not delivered.

During all this time, I was in denial and was in communications exile. The superficial Dr. Phil role I was playing was just a ruse to cover my own pain. I was really in deep depression and despair, and I was the one who needed someone who I could talk to about my issues. However, I didn't feel I could talk to my wife. The Devil told me she didn't care about my mother or me; and unfortunately, I believed what he said. I believed it even though I've always known that the Devil is a liar. Ironically, even when I did want to talk to my wife, it was either bad timing or she didn't seem to be interested. So this is where the enemy really began to work. Once again, he exploited an area of weakness. In his typical seductive way, he told me to open up to these women. Satan was not interested in me getting any better, because he knew that these unsaved women could not help me – but they could help him destroy me.

Before I go any further, I want to make this crystal clear. My wife is not the one who is at fault here and neither am I blaming her for any of my non-sexual, but emotional infidelities. I am at fault for allowing the enemy to deceive me and use me.

Once I began confiding in these women, they knew how to say all the right things. One day while at home on my computer, I received an instant message from an on-line acquaintance. The woman on the other end started telling me about how she was having an affair with a married man. This should have been a major red-flag, but it tweaked my interest so I engaged her and we began an online chat. The next thing I knew, she started going into graphic details about her sexual encounters with her adulterous lover. After she finished, it was my turn. So I traded a steamy story as well of a sexual escapade that I had with my wife. My intentions were to appeal to her by appearing to be just as erotic and wild as she was. However, I did not reveal the fact that the encounter I was describing occurred between my wife and I. After the chat ended, I signed off and shut down the computer.

Later on that evening, my wife was on the computer and somehow the instant message conversation that I had earlier popped up, and my wife saw it. After reading it, she was livid because she thought I was having an affair. There was no way for her to know that I was actually describing an encounter between me and her, because I intentionally left out her name. She also thought I had several other affairs during our marriage, but this was not true. I have never had an affair outside of my marriage! And the fact that we were having some communication problems only fed her incorrect suspicions. However, in her mind, this message that she found was all the confirmation that she needed. In anger, my wife printed several copies of this conversation and she told our children about it and threatened to divorce me.

During this time, I had a part-time job and after my shift, I returned home around 4:30 in the morning. I got into the bed with her (not knowing that she had read this conversation or anything) and held her in my arms until she awoke that next morning. I was still in the bed asleep while she had gotten all the kids off to school and she was getting ready for work. Usually she would allow me to stay asleep until after she had left, and call me on her way to work. However, this morning she stayed and asked me to wake up. Her exact words were, "Baby, wake up. You have been cheating on me and you are going to pay. I know all about your women. I read your email and I'm going to tell everybody you know." I pleaded with her over and over again, trying to tell her that I had never actually cheated, but that those were just words in an email conversation. I begged her not to do anything she would regret the rest of her life. We continued the argument for several more minutes. She was unrelenting, and did not believe anything I said.

Since we were unable to reconcile at the time, I had to

move in with my sister Shelia and her husband Alvin. I began to realize the pain and suffering my wife must have gone through all those years we were not communicating. This spirit of bitterness must have been with her a long time; however, it was my fault. It was because of my own unresolved issues that a wedge was forced between us. My dear wife never asked for this or did anything to bring this situation about. I accept full blame for contributing to her state. Since I was the one who was withdrawn and isolative, I created an environment for those spirits to dominate my life.

It is very important to understand that the enemy always wants to get you isolated so he may have his way with you. He doesn't want you to get help and support from those who love you. He wants you alone, so he can manipulate you into doing his bidding without any resistance from the righteous. Not only does he not want you to be in fellowship with people who love you, he doesn't want you to be in fellowship with the Lord, who is the only one who can deliver you from his wicked schemes.

Chapter 6

The Time Bomb Exploded!

    While I was immersed in all my issues, my wife was also going through something even more intense. No, my wife did not start having affairs to get back at me, but she did have to deal with all of her toxic emotions from my dysfunctions. When you add depression, hurt, anger, and jealously, and mix them together within the confines of a marital relationship, you can have an extremely volatile situation. This is exactly how those crimes of passion happen, when one person seemingly snaps. Unfortunately, too many circumstances like these end up in tragedy. For example, there was a case not too long ago where a couple had been struggling in their marriage for years. One day, the wife had enough, snapped and killed her husband. She tied him down to the bed, stabbed him one-hundred and ninety three times, and then buried him in the back yard.

It is very important when you are in love with someone and feelings of anger, hurt and jealousy come on you, that you do not write them off as just "feelings." Since all of us have a flesh nature, even though we may be born again, we must be careful to not allow the enemy to take advantage of us by exploiting the weaknesses that we all have in our flesh. The Apostle Paul warns us in Romans 7:18 "For I know that in me (that is, in my flesh,) dwelleth no good thing." He also warns that we have no confidence in the flesh (Philippians 3:3). Whenever we get too angry, too depressed, too anxious, too tired, too lonely, too hungry, or too anything, we are open to being exploited by demonic forces that lay in wait for such an opportunity. So our emotions are not just mere "feelings," but are the gateways for wickedness to enter.

For example, hate is an intense feeling of dislike and anger. It is akin to hatred, which is in the Galatians 5 list of the works of the flesh. However, hatred is a gateway to other spirits. For example, In 1 John, the bible says:

> He that saith he is in the light, and hateth his brother, is in darkness even until now.... But he that hateth his brother is in darkness, and walketh in darkness, and knoweth not whither he goeth, because that darkness hath blinded his eyes,
> 1 John 2:9 and 11

In these passages, we find the phrases "is in darkness," and "walketh in darkness." In both cases, they can be tied to demonic influences. This we know from Ephesians 6, where one of the names Paul uses for demons is "the rulers of the darkness." Notice that this demonic darkness causes spiritual blindness and causes a person to be led into dark places where he "knoweth not whither he goeth." Spiritual blindness is clearly caused by Satan and his demons (2 Corinthians 4:4).

Next, 1 John tells us that hate is the gateway to another spirit: *murder.* The passage reads, "Whosoever hateth his brother is a murderer: and ye know that no murderer hath eternal life abiding in him (1 John 3:15). This is the same spirit that rose up in Cain, who killed his brother Abel because he hated his brother, who offered an acceptable sacrifice unto the Lord. His *hate* opened the door for *murder.* Clearly, the bible teaches that if you are a hater, you are also a murderer, because you are open to that spirit.

A final example of a spirit that follows hate is a *lying spirit.* Notice what John also says, "If a man say, I love God, and hateth his brother, he is a liar..." (1 John 4:20). In many cases, hate will attempt to disguise itself under the cloak of love, but in reality, a lying spirit is in operation. Remember, it was Judas who betrayed the Lord with a kiss, an expression of love. Hate will have people smiling in your face, while stabbing you in your back. So the lying spirit comes to disguise their hate, to get them close enough to hurt you. Individuals who cannot stand you do not always make their feelings obvious. From all of this biblical evidence, we can clearly see that there is a lot more to hate than just the mere feeling.

Whenever you are confronted with bad feelings, it is important to quickly find someone and get help. Talk to someone. Find someone and pray together. Do not keep these emotions inside. It is the Devil's desire that you keep everything in the dark, because he works well in darkness. In order to manipulate you, he will tell you, "No one else understands. Those church people don't know anything. They all have their own issues."

Another subtle move the Devil will often make is if you are determined to get help, he will steer you towards ungodly counsel. The Devil does not want you to hear the truth, because he knows that the bible teaches that the truth shall make you free (John 8:32). Additionally, the Devil does not want you to be blessed either, because of what the bible says in the first Psalm:

> Blessed *is* the man that walketh not in the counsel of the ungodly, nor standeth in the way of sinners, nor sitteth in the seat of the scornful. But his delight *is* in the law of the LORD; and in his law doth he meditate day and night. And he shall be like a tree planted by the rivers of water, that bringeth forth his fruit in his season; his leaf also shall not wither; and whatsoever he doeth shall prosper. The ungodly *are* not so: but *are* like the chaff which the wind driveth away. Therefore the ungodly shall not stand in the judgment, nor sinners in the congregation of the righteous. For the LORD knoweth the way of the righteous: but the way of the ungodly shall perish.
>
> Psalms 1:1-6

Run For Your Life!

While at my sister's house, it was a very difficult time for me. I cried every night and wished that I was dead. I wished I had died with my mother. I would lie in their basement many nights wishing that when I go to sleep, I wouldn't wake up. However, I did wake up. Day after day, no matter what, I'd wake up again. It's amazing that you can become so despondent that you will desire, even pray, that God let you die. We see that this was the case with even the prophet Elijah. After Jezebel had threatened to kill him, Elijah had reached such a level of despair that this powerful prophet asked the Lord to take his life. Here is what the prophet said:

> But he himself went a day's journey into the wilderness, and came and sat down under a juniper tree: and he requested for himself that he might die; and said, It is enough; now, O LORD, take away my life; for I am not better than my fathers.
>
> I Kings 19:4

However, God will not let you die when He has a work for you to do. While I was going through separation from my wife, my sister and brother-in-law graciously let me stay at their home. I also stayed one month at my godparents' home as well. While at my sister Shelia's house, Sylvia (my other sister) would come by to encourage and pray for me. Slowly but surely, my desire to live again returned. Soon, I gained the courage to face and defeat my demons. While there, I had time to think, pray and ask God for forgiveness. I lamented for many days. And I pleaded with the Lord to forgive me for allowing the enemy to have his way with me. In being so disobedient to God, I was really putting Christ to open shame. That really broke my heart. The Lord who died for me, I was putting him to open shame through my actions.

While recuperating, I had time to hear God. On the nights when I wasn't able to sleep, I spent most of the night in prayer. On many occasions, I could hear the Lord say, "I have forgiven you. I've called and ordained you to accomplish all of the work that I have purposed for you to do. Be of good courage my son, and live."

Even though I had already been made the pastor of the church, looking back at it, I was still running from my assignment. The church was growing with new members, and the people were excited about the new visions. The church was growing financially and it was a new chapter in our church's history. However, I was still meeting some opposition that was wearing on me. On several occasions, I was openly criticized in the church. There were some in the congregation who were unhappy with how I was running the church. People started murmuring and complaining behind my back and criticizing me to my face. Many of the plans I had brought before the church were blocked.

By this time, I was tired of fighting for every inch of progress. I told the Lord I was only going to serve as pastor for one more year. That would be the last year of "my five year plan." I had had it! I simply could not take it anymore. I had too many battlefronts to maintain. I had been going through depression for years, and had to confront problems in the church. All of this stress exacerbated the emotional trauma I was contending with internally from the passing of my mother. It was like my life was being lived out in a small room where the walls were closing in on me. I had to get out.

One morning while at my sister and brother-in-law's home, I was watching the religious channel. The program was Dr. Hilliard. Dr. Hilliard was preaching on how God has a work for you to do, and often times we want to do it our way or not at all. Dr. Hilliard said God has to get your attention to get you to do what He wants you to do. He said, "God puts things like sickness, death, and trouble in your life to get your attention. Then he said, "God will put you flat on your back, to say to you 'can you hear me now?'" Those words pierced my soul like a two edged sword. I will never forget those timely words. Right there as I laid in the bed, I was moved to tears. Then by divine providence, the next program that came on was Dr. Juanita Bynum. She began to preach the same type of message that Dr. Hilliard had just preached, that God has a way of getting your attention.

Dr. Bynum began to expound to the people and her television audience as if she were talking directly to me. She began saying that many times God can't talk to you while you're unfocused and running here and there. God has to put you down, and while you're down, He'll ask you, "Can you hear me now?" When she said this, I leaped out the bed! I began crying and praising God. I said, "Yes Lord, I hear you! I hear you! I hear you now!" This initiated my complete recovery and my complete deliverance. Not only had I been bound by sex and depression, I also had a spirit of rebellion and running from the Lord. I realized that these were all works of flesh. The flesh only wants constant pleasure, but can never be satisfied. Therefore the flesh has to die. We have to crucify the flesh and the deeds thereof. As it says in Galatians 5:24, "And they that are Christ's have crucified the flesh with the affections and lusts." In Ephesians 2:2-3, the Word of God tells us:

> Wherein in time past ye walked according to the course of this world, according to the prince of the power of the air, the spirit that now worketh in the children of disobedience: Among whom also we all had our conversation in times past in the lusts of our flesh, fulfilling the desires of the flesh and of the mind; and were by nature the children of wrath, even as others.

This is a real battle that we must fight daily. The flesh (our fallen, sinful nature) always wants to be in control. You must pray daily and fast when necessary. These are ways to keep the flesh from rising up and controlling your soul. Whichever one you feed the most, whether it be the flesh or the spirit man, is the one that will dominate. Therefore, we must feed our inner man and starve the flesh. However, the more you give in to the dictates of your flesh, it's the same as feeding the flesh. It then becomes stronger, and it becomes harder for you to defeat the power of strongholds.

After hearing these words, my eyes were opened. Then the Lord completely delivered me. I could feel the Holy Spirit moving inside of me as never before. I was renewed in the spirit of my mind and transformed into a new creation in Christ Jesus. Though I struggled for years, in an instant, the Lord had released me from the shackles of the Devil. He made all things work together for my good. Now that I had experienced what real deliverance was about, I could tell others. Now I have a more perfect understanding of what the bible says in Revelation 12:11: And they overcame him by the blood of the Lamb, and by the word of their testimony. This was my new charge given to me by the Lord, to be a witness against all manner of evil and strongholds.

While at my godparents' home, the Lord opened the lines of communications between me and my wife. At first I started off by writing letters to her. I still didn't know if she had forgiven me or believed that I was delivered. However, one day my wife sent me a scrumptious home-cooked meal. I didn't realize how much I missed her cooking until I began to dig into that smothered baked chicken, with rice and gravy, and vegetables on the side. Oh my God, this was the best meal I had ever had! Not only did her cooking satisfy my appetite, but the love she put into it filled my heart with joy. I then knew she had forgiven me and was ready to accept me back into her life.

Once she decided to reconcile, I didn't want to rush anything, so we started off at a slow pace. We first began to go out on dates. Then she brought the children over and we spent the day together as a family, then they spent the night with me. It wasn't long after that the Lord reunited us and reaffirmed our marriage, and we have been together ever since. We are stronger. We are better than before. We are wiser. We are one. We are the husband and wife, we are the family, and we are the church that God called us to be. Thank God for his Deliverance!

Chapter 7

Stronghold Spirits

In this chapter, I will be identifying the stronghold spirits and demons which can live in us and overtake our souls. These stronghold spirits are listed by groups to help us better understand how spirits set themselves up in groups to get a greater stronghold on your soul. In the eleventh chapter of the Gospel of Luke, Jesus explains the progressive nature of demonic possession by saying:

> When the unclean spirit is gone out of a man, he walketh through dry places, seeking rest; and finding none, he saith, I will return unto my house whence I came out. And when he cometh, he findeth *it* swept and garnished. Then goeth he, and taketh *to him* seven other spirits more wicked than himself; and they enter in, and dwell

there: and the last *state* of that man is worse than the first.

Luke 11:24-26

Whenever they can, demons will enter into a person in succession and even in great numbers, as was the case with the demoniac at Gadara (see Luke 8:30). In order for demons to operate in the earth realm, they need a host body to express themselves – preferably human, but in rare cases animals will do as well (see Luke 8:33).

Understanding the spirits and demons that are on you is one of the first steps towards your deliverance. I listed these stronghold spirits in groups to show how these spirits work. These spirits do not come alone. The Devil wants to destroy you. The thief comes not but for to steal, and to kill and to destroy. The enemy will never send only one spirit because he knows that the spirit in man is more powerful.

I want you to look at this list, and circle all those spirits that are associated with you and your life. You should focus on this and work on this spirit, and ask God for your complete deliverance. Focus on you, and ask God to help you. When you have finished reading this book; please pass it on and help someone else.

Stronghold Spirits

ACCUSATION
Criticism
Faultfinding
Judging

BITTERNESS
Anger
Hatred
Murder
Resentment
Retaliation
Temper
Unforgiving
Violence

CONTROL
Dominance
Possessiveness
Witchcraft
Rape

HEAVINESS
Burden
Disgust
Gloom

REBELLION
Disobedience
Self-willed
Stubbornness
Quarrelling

STRIFE
Argument
Bickering
Contention
Fighting

ESCAPE
Alcohol
Drugs
Sleepiness
Indifference
Passivity
Sleepiness
Stoicism

DEPRESSION
Death
Defeatism
Dejection
Despair
Despondency
Discouragement
Hopelessness
Insomnia
Suicide

JEALOUSY
Distrust
Envy
Selfishness
Suspicion

REJECTION
Fear of Rejection
Self-rejection
Separation Anxiety

Spirits of Error
False Doctrine
Heresy
Occultism
Magic
Astrology
False Prophesy

PASSIVITY
Funk
Indifference
Lethargy
Lethargy
Listlessness

INSECURITY
Inadequacy
Ineptness
Inferiority
Loneliness
Self-Pity
Shyness
Spit
Timidity

LUST
Homosexuality
Perversion
Hypersexual
Fornication
Adultery
Child Molestation
Pornography

RETALIATION
Destruction
Hatred
Sadism

WITHDRAWAL
Daydreaming
Fantasy
Pouting
Pretension
Unreality

Anatomy of a Stronghold

Now that I have completed telling my own story of how the enemy almost destroyed my life, my marriage, my family and my ministry, it is time to switch the focus from me to those of you who need to know how to be overcomers in Christ Jesus. For it is only through the power of his Spirit, his Word, his armor and his weapons that we can experience total freedom and walk in the assurance that we are more than conquerors. However, knowing these things is not enough. Not only must we know them, we must understand them and live by them. There is a big difference between knowing that an airplane can fly and understanding how to fly an airplane. Merely knowing something is limited to superficial head knowledge, and can be achieved in an instance of time. However, having a complete understanding of something only comes from years of study, training and experience, which is often riddled with trial and error.

So when it comes to standing up against the powers of darkness, we cannot approach such a serious subject with a television mentally. There are no silver bullets, wooden stakes or strings of garlic that can ward off demons. These are real supernatural powers that only respect one thing – the power of God. This is why the Apostle Paul was careful to instruct the Corinthians in this matter:

> For though we walk in the flesh, we do not war after the flesh: (For the weapons of our warfare *are* not carnal, but mighty through God to the pulling down of strong holds;) Casting down imaginations, and every high thing that exalteth

itself against the knowledge of God, and bringing into captivity every thought to the obedience of Christ.

2 Corinthians 10:3-5

In chapter one, we learned a functional definition for stronghold, that it is basically a term that pertains to warfare and military terminology. We discussed that a stronghold occurred when a territory was captured by the enemy and used as a staging point to initiate and facilitate further attacks. For example, in 1 Samuel 17:1, the passage reads:

> Now the Philistines gathered together their armies to battle, and were gathered together at Shochoh, which belongeth to Judah, and pitched between Shochoh and Azekah, in Ephes-dammim.

This campaign set the stage for the Philistines to send out Goliath, their giant warrior, who evoked tremendous fear amongst the people of Israel. However, what I want to point out here is the fact that they pitched, or set up, camp in a place that originally belonged to Judah, but was now seized by the Philistines. It was from this seized place that the Philistines launched their weapon, Goliath, to seek to defeat and bring Israel into captivity and bondage.

Once the enemy captured a territory or city, they used everything in their arsenal to maintain control of that place. In other words, once they moved in, their intentions were to stay. And from that very place that they have taken, they continue to take more, so they can maintain, harass and control, until they have completely conquered their opposition. This is the essence of a physical military stronghold. However, when we speak of strongholds in the spiritual sense, these are areas of our lives that have been yielded to the enemy, places where he digs in and launches his attacks in order to bring and keep a person in bondage until he has completely destroyed that individual.

The main differences between military strongholds and spiritual ones are the battlefield, the weapons used and the warfare tactics. When dealing with spiritual strongholds and spiritual warfare, the battlefield is the mind. In many places in the bible, the word "heart" is often used, but it is actually synonymous with the mind. For example, the bible says, "For as he thinketh in his heart, so is he" (Proverbs 23:7). Clearly we can understand that our actual heart is a muscle that pumps blood throughout our body's vascular system.

Our physical heart has no capacity to think, as the above passage suggests. Clearly, what is meant here is the mind, which is the seat of thoughts, imaginations and knowledge. This is why in the only instance of the word stronghold in the New Testament, it is in reference to activities that occur in the mind. Now this is not to suggest that a person cannot be actually possessed by a demon, because the bible clearly teaches that this does occur. However, when we speak of strongholds, though they may be demonically inspired, their main theatre of operation begins in our minds.

As we look again to 2 Corinthians 10:3-5, there are three areas of attack specifically targeted by the enemy. They are imaginations, knowledge and thoughts, all which are functions of our metaphoric heart, which is actually our mind. In order for us to effectively fend off an attack of the enemy, we must become proficient in casting down imaginations. Some time ago, there was a well known evangelist who said, "You may not be able to stop a bird from flying over your head, but you can stop him from landing and building a nest on your head." In other words, you may not be able to always control all the information that enters your mind, but you can control what you do with that information. The scriptures tell us that if we are to be successful in pulling down strongholds through the power of God, we must first cast down those imaginations.

Years ago in the late 1960's, there was a song that had this line in it: "well it was just my imagination, running away with me." Ironically, this song was sung by the "Temptations," and that is exactly how temptation works - it starts with an imagination that begins to run wild in your mind. Without the power to *cast down* that imagination, you will act out on what you are imagining. As soon as you decide to act out on this imagination, your flesh kicks in, because that imagination needs your flesh to fulfill and manifest the lust thereof. Here is where the problem gets even deeper.

As the bible clearly tells us, in our flesh dwells no good thing. It also tells us that we were all born and shaped in iniquity, so we already have the evil within us. However, the flesh needs an imagination to be in agreement with, so together they act in concert to manifest and act out the lust that would otherwise lay dormant. This is why in James 1:14-15, it says, "But every man is tempted, when he is drawn away of his own lust, and enticed. Then when lust hath conceived, it bringeth forth sin: and sin, when it is finished, bringeth forth death." The *drawing away* here is in reference to the powerful enticement of an imagination that has not been cast down.

A perfect example of an imagination gone wild is what happened to King David. In his case, the imagination entered in through his eyes. Once he saw beautiful naked Bathsheba bathing on her terrace, that was all it took for him to act out on his imagination of having sex with her. And we know where this story turns up. David ended up in an adulterous relationship, committing murder, and the child from that adulterous union died. However, it didn't stop there. Evil rose up in his own family. His daughter Tamar was raped by her own brother, Amnon. David's other son Absalom killed Amnon for raping Tamar. And then Absalom ended up leading a rebellion against David and fleeing from Jerusalem. Since Absalom was a rebel, he was caught and executed by David's army, which further broke David's heart. All these consequences, which started with one unchecked imagination, almost destroyed a nation. If David were here now, he would testify that that was one imagination he wished he would have cast down.

One of today's popular slogans used by the United Negro College Fund is, "A mind is a terrible thing to waste." It is true! In Proverbs 4:23, we are warned when it says, "Keep thy heart with all diligence; for out of it are the issues of life." In other words, be very careful about what you allow to enter into your mind, because it's from your mind that all your issues flow. All of your thoughts, desires, wishes, hopes, dreams, talents, emotions, temperament, personality and character are all functions of your mind and soul. Your soul is what makes you – you.

We all basically have the same bodies, in regards to general characteristics such as having a head, two eyes, two ears, a nose, a mouth, two arms, two legs, etc. However, we are vastly different when it comes to our souls. Once information enters our mind, it becomes a part of our soul. This is a good thing if all the information you put in your soul is good. However, once you know something, you cannot unknow it – it's in there forever. There are no delete buttons, like on a computer keyboard, that you can hit, and the information is gone forever. Once information goes in, it has the potential to change you for better or for worse.

This is what happened to Adam and Eve. As long as they obeyed God and had not eaten from the tree of the knowledge of good and evil, they were fine. But once the knowledge of evil entered, they were changed forever. The first thing that happened after they ate was that their eyes were opened to the darkness of sin. Darkness then, became their light. What had been beautiful immediately became shameful. And the God whom they fellowshipped with during the cool of the day, they now hid from because they were afraid of him. The knowledge of evil polluted their minds and souls. Everything that emanated out from that soul was irreversibly tainted by sin. The knowledge of sin now works as a principle in the earth realm. Paul refers to it in Romans 8:2, as "the law of sin and death."

In 1 Peter 2:11, the Apostle gives us this solemn warning: "Dearly beloved, I beseech you as strangers and pilgrims, abstain from fleshly lusts, which war against the soul." As I just stated, you cannot unknow what you know. Once you experience something, that thing gets into your soul and takes root in your mind. If the wrong things get into your mind, by way of the five senses or by way of participation, these things war against your soul to bring it into bondage. That first high. That first drink. That first gambling experience. That first sexual encounter. No matter what it is, it goes in through your mind, and wars against your soul, eventually becoming a stronghold that will dominate you until it completely destroys you.

Psychological Effects of Demonic Strongholds

Any type of abuse is enormously destructive, and it is particularly devastating when you perpetrate it on a child. A child has no defenses against the mental and emotional scars that abuse leaves behind. Once they are sexualized, they cannot turn it off. They cannot unknow what they know. And that thing, that stronghold, that demon, lurks in their mind and becomes a part of their soul, until their identity and character are shaped by the abuse that they experienced. It is a terrible sin to abuse a child. This is why Jesus says, "But whoso shall offend one of these little ones which believe in me, it were better for him that a millstone were hanged about his neck, and that he were drowned in the depth of the sea" (Matthew 18:6). More often than not, the abusee becomes the abuser. This is the ultimate expression of a stronghold spirit - the person becomes the very thing that they hate. Most prostitutes, homosexuals, pedophiles and rapists were at one time abused by someone they knew and trusted.

The long range effects of any type of dysfunction,

whether it is sexual abuse, substance abuse, physical abuse, or any type of destructive behavior, plays out in all areas of the victim's life. For example, if a child comes up in a family where the father is an alcoholic, the entire family must make adjustments to accommodate the father's dysfunction. If dad is too drunk to work and be the man of the house, this will fall unto the eldest child, perhaps the eldest son. Let's say this happens when the young man is only twelve years old. Now he becomes the man of the house. This is called an informal role. He's mama's "little man" who can take care of things. This is what is called a parental child, who through dysfunctional circumstances is pushed into adult responsibilities. However in doing so, he also becomes the hero of the family. He's the man of the house, who can help mama with running the house. He can step up to the plate and take care of things.

While all this responsibility builds up his young ego, as being the one that the family can depend on, it also puts him in direct opposition to his father, because in many cases, he is filling in for his father. An emotional wedge of disrespect begins to be forged. So as the hero of the family, he must rescue his mother and his younger siblings from his father's alcoholic episodes. This pre-adolescent's personality has been altered because of the adjustments the family had to make due to the father's alcoholism. The problem is that although he is called mama's little man and he's likes being the hero who can rescue, he is a child, who should not be in those roles. He, too, is hurting on the inside and is emotionally scarred, though his ego is being stroked by dysfunctional circumstances.

Unbeknownst to him, he has been imprinted with a

hero/rescuer mindset that is dysfunctional and illegitimate. Since he never had a normal childhood, emotionally he stopped growing at twelve when the dysfunction started. So now that he is thirty, he can't understand why he keeps having failed relationships. He doesn't understand why he keeps selecting women who have so many issues and need rescuing. He can't figure out why he always finds himself in situations where he can be seen as the hero. He doesn't understand why he is so impulsive and makes poor decisions, and why he is so emotionally unbalanced and immature. Although, he is thirty years old chronologically, emotionally he's still only twelve years old.

Not understanding why he is in so much pain, he attempts to medicate himself, and reaches out for alcohol, just like his father, or drugs. And once again, the cycle repeats itself, to effect and destroy another generation. Everything this young man does in his adult life is done through the lens of the dysfunctional role forced upon him as a child. Everything from the mate he will chose to the career he will pursue, must allow him to function in that hero's role. However, it is important to understand that he will not consciously seek this role; it's all sub-conscious. He will do it without even thinking about it. This is because the same stronghold spirit that tormented his father now torments him. This is one of the ways the scripture is fulfilled when it instructs, "...and that will by no means clear the guilty; visiting the iniquity of the fathers upon the children, and upon the children's children, unto the third and to the fourth generation" (Exodus 34:7). Strongholds are very serious business.

Chapter 8

Demons

As we covered earlier, there are many names that are given to describe the invisible forces of spiritual wickedness. Behind heinous acts of evil perpetrated by humans, there are diabolical supernatural powers of darkness called demons. In Matthew 25:41, the bible tells us:

> Then shall he say also unto them on the left hand, Depart from me, ye cursed, into everlasting fire, prepared for the Devil and his angels.

In this passage, we learn that demons are fallen angelic beings. This means that they have similar powers as do the holy angels. They are immortal, invisible, supernatural, intelligent, powerful and immeasurably evil. At some time in eternity past, all of the angelic beings, which includes Lucifer (the Devil's pre-fallen name), were holy angels. It was only after there was a rebellion in heaven, prior to the creation of the earth, that one third of the heavenly host followed Satan and were cast out of heaven and became what the bible calls demons. We get a metaphorical picture of this in Revelation 12: 3-4, where it says:

> And there appeared another wonder in heaven; and behold a great red dragon, having seven heads and ten horns, and seven crowns upon his heads. And his tail drew the third part of the stars of heaven, and did cast them to the earth...

From this passage, we learn that whatever the total number of angels is, one-third of them followed Satan. That means there are countless millions of demons. Jude also refers to demons as "the angels that left their first estate" (Jude 6). They are also referred to as unclean spirits that cause sickness, diseases, physical maladies, madness, all sorts of sexual perversion. They inspire evil behavior and actions in human beings. Under the right conditions, demons are also allowed to completely possess human beings. No human being in his own power is a match for these demonic spirits.

Demons are also behind idol worship. In 1 Corinthians, the Apostle Paul warns:

> But I say, that the things which the Gentiles sacrifice, they sacrifice to Devils, and not to God: and I would not that ye should have fellowship with Devils. Ye cannot drink the cup of the Lord,

and the cup of Devils: ye cannot be partakers of the Lord's table, and of the table of Devils.
1Cor.10:20-21

Not only do demons inspire idol worship, they are also the source of false doctrine and heresy. The Apostle Paul gives a characteristic of the end-times, where demon-influenced ministers will teach damnable doctrines:

> Now the Spirit speaketh expressly, that in the latter times some shall depart from the faith, giving heed to seducing spirits, and doctrines of Devils; Speaking lies in hypocrisy; having their conscience seared with a hot iron.
> I Timothy 4:1

Unfortunately, because of Hollywood films and television, people think Devils appear as ugly hideous creatures. However, nothing could be further from the truth. The bible tells us that even Satan himself is transformed into an angel of light, so that he may deceive (2 Corinthians 11:14). His whole purpose is to exploit human weakness through his power to seduce and entice. Unfortunately, one of the greatest tools in his arsenal is to work through people without them knowing that he's there.

Soul-Ties

Another way strongholds enter into our lives is through the ungodly *soul-tie,* therefore, it is necessary to cover this topic briefly. Soul-ties can either be godly or ungodly. A soul-tie is when there is a deep attachment to another individual, by way of friendship, intimate relationship, or other strong involvement with that person. As a matter of fact, the bible actually uses the terms "knitted together" or "cleave to" to express the idea of two individuals who are stuck together like glue. The first inference of a soul-tie in the bible is found in the second chapter of Genesis, where the bible speaks of the marital relationship. The text reads:

> Therefore shall a man leave his father and his mother, and shall cleave unto his wife: and they shall be one flesh.
> Genesis 2:24

Just about anyone who is married can tell you about soul-ties. When the souls of two people are knitted together, they often think the same thoughts at the same time and can even complete one another's sentences. They can feel what their spouse is feeling, even when they are not in close proximity. They can know things about one another, because as the bible says they shall be one flesh. In other words, though there are two people, in the eyes of God they are one because their hearts (their souls) are knitted together. The secular idea of this concept is referred to as a soul-mate.

Godly soul-ties are not limited to the martial relationship only, because best of friends can have a soul-tie as well. We find such a friendship soul-tie with the relationship between Jonathan and David. In 1 Samuel 18:1 and 3 the bible says:

> And it came to pass, when he had made an end

of speaking unto Saul, that the soul of Jonathan was knit with the soul of David, and Jonathan loved him as his own soul.... Then Jonathan and David made a covenant, because he loved him as his own soul.

In this passage, we learn that the soul of Jonathan was "knit" with the soul of David, and that Jonathan loved David as his own soul. Deep brotherly love was the basis or the glue that bonded their souls together. So whenever there is deep love for someone, the potential for a soul-tie exists. In many cases, soul-ties are confirmed with a vow or covenant. In the case of Jonathan and David, a covenant. In the case of a married couple, a wedding vow. As long as the friendship or love between the individuals is not self-centered or tainted with manipulation or control, the soul-ties are healthy and mutually beneficial. People who are soul-tied cannot just simply walk away from each other, because the root of their tie is too deep. Even if they go through difficulties, they can have no rest until they clear up their issues and reconcile. Again, this holds true for platonic relationships as well as martial relationships.

Soul-ties can also develop between the pastor and members of a congregation. Often, member of a congregation will have the same spirit as their pastor. In the church setting, extremely close bonds can develop. For example, in 1 Corinthians, the Apostle Paul teaches,

Now I beseech you, brethren, by the name of our Lord Jesus Christ, that ye all speak the same thing, and that there be no divisions among you; but that ye be perfectly joined together in the same mind and in the same judgment.

1 Corinthians 1:10

Healthy soul-ties in the church benefit the whole congregation by helping to fight against division, factions, false doctrine. However, if there are ungodly soul-ties that are allowed to fester in the church, the pastor can end up with too much power and control over the people. Extreme cases can end up like the People's Church in Jonestown, where Jim Jones lead over nine-hundred people to their deaths.

Ungodly Soul-Ties

There is a very important question found in Amos 3:3: can two walk together, except they be agreed? In order for a soul-tie to be formed, there has to be some type of agreement. There has to be some type of coming together. There has to be some type of sticking together or bonding. However, it is also important to understand that not all "coming together," "sticking together" or "cleaving together" is appropriate, healthy or for mutual benefit. In the cases where there is a controlling spirit that simply wants to dominate others, this is an *ungodly* soul-tie. Ultimately, ungodly soul-ties are very destructive and quickly lay the foundation for the stronghold.

If we go back to our definition of a stronghold, we stated that it is a place that the enemy seizes, where he launches attacks to defeat and bring someone under his control. When the enemy is obvious, we are quicker to be on our guard. However, when we do not recognize the enemy, that's much harder to defend against. Therefore, the Devil will use the power of the ungodly soul-tie to set up his stronghold. Remember, soul-ties are based on agreement, whether it be love-based agreement or friendship-based agreement. This is why who you are in agreement with is so important.

One of the main areas that ungodly soul-ties occur is through illicit sexual contact. For example, when the bible speaks of the married couple, "the two becoming one flesh," this is in reference to the union that brings both people together at a soulish, even spiritual, level through the physical act of sex. The bliss of sexual intercourse is how God knits both your souls together. In the context of marriage, the bed is undefiled (Hebrews 13:4). However, the bible warns against illicit sexual contact.

> ... Know ye not that your bodies are the members of Christ? shall I then take the members of Christ, and make them the members of an harlot? God forbid. What? know ye not that he which is joined to an harlot is one body? for two, saith he, shall be one flesh. But he that is joined unto the Lord is one spirit. Flee fornication. Every sin that a man doeth is without the body; but he that committeth fornication sinneth against his own body.
>
> 1 Corinthians 6:14-18

In Paul's strong admonition to the Corinthians, he makes a salient point by asking this rhetorical question: shall I then take the members of Christ, and make them the members of an harlot? His sharp response is, "God forbid!" The NIV translates his response as "Never!" The reason this drew such a pointed response from the apostle was because of what he says next. "Know ye not that he which is joined to an harlot is one body? for two, saith he, shall be one flesh." Herein is the danger. The word harlot means prostitute. As we all know, a prostitute sleeps with many different people, both male and female. Each time she or he has sexual intercourse with one of the customers, she or he is joining souls with each one of these people. When prostitute and a "john" come together, not only are they sharing diseases, but strongholds or demonic spirits can transfer between them as well.

The person having sex with the prostitute is then soul-tied to the prostitute, whose soul is full of evil transference from all the other souls with whom she or he has had relations. This is a very serious issue because after a person has slept with a prostitute and then goes home and sleeps with his or her spouse, the spouse can now also be polluted from these toxic relationships, unaware. Even in the physical sense, when you sleep with some, you are sleeping with all of the other people that she or he has slept with. This is how the enemy spreads deadly sexually transmitted disease, through illicit sexual contact.

Ungodly soul-ties can also be developed between any two people who are open to one another. However, the strength of the soul-tie depends upon how deeply you are involved with the other person's heart. You can be soul-tied to relatives, close friends, co-workers and even the leadership you are under, whether it be secular or spiritual. The level of solidarity that we have with others is evidence of the intensity of the soul-tie. Have you ever seen a situation where a man physically abuses a woman, yet she will not leave him? Have you ever seen a person who is a member of a church where the leadership dogs them, yet they won't leave? This is all evidence of a soul-tie. Even though the victim knows that they are being abused and that the relationship is toxic, they still will not consider breaking the relationship, and will even turn against you for suggesting it. If they did get to the point where they want to sever the relationship, they won't because they don't believe that they can leave or they don't believe they can survive without the abuser.

As I stated earlier, the battlefield is in the mind. We also covered that our emotions, our will, our personalities, etc. are all functions of the soul, and what one thinks in his heart controls who he is. To illustrate this point further, let me tell you about the elephant and the chain. Once there was a traveler who visited an African country where elephants were used for labor. He noticed that these humongous elephants were being kept in place by this relatively small chain. He couldn't help but notice that with one simple move of their head, they could have easily pulled up the stake in the ground to which the chain was attached. The traveler marveled, and asked the elephant trainer, "Why don't they pull up the stake to get free?" The trainer responded, "They don't think that they can do it, so they don't try."

The trainer went on to explain that the elephants were conditioned when they were young. When the elephants were babies, they were not strong enough to pull up the stake that secures the chain. The young elephants did resist, but they soon learned they couldn't break free. After a while, they stopped trying, because they knew they couldn't do it. That conditioning stays with them throughout their life. Once they become adults, they actually have the strength to easily break the chain or pull up the stake, but they don't because when they there were young, their minds had been preconditioned to believe that they could not get free. So as adults, they don't try because they believe that the chain is still stronger than they are.

Though I'm not trying to say that the elephants were soul-tied, this analogy was only important in emphasizing the fact that although soul-ties are powerful weapons of the enemy, in order for him to get them to work, he needs you to empower the soul-tie with your own belief. In other words, the enemy will use your "disbelief" (I can't break the chain) to become your "belief" (the chain can't be broken) in order to give power to his lie. Remember, though soul-ties and strongholds are demonically inspired, they are still illegitimate and based upon a lie. Therefore, they can all be broken and destroyed through the truth and the power of God's Spirit.

The bible tells us in Proverbs 4:7, "Wisdom is the principal thing; therefore get wisdom: and with all thy getting get understanding." In everything we do, we need wisdom and understanding. Much of remaining free from strongholds, soul-ties and another forms of spiritual attack that we encounter is by simply using wisdom.

Thought it is said in the world and even in the church that "experience is the best teacher," I would beg to differ with that idiom. When it comes to driving a car, yes, experience is the best teacher. You will never learn how to drive on Chicago's Dan Ryan Expressway just by using some driving simulator. In order to become a proficient driver, you have to get out there in the traffic. However, when it comes to many other things, wisdom is the best teacher. Wisdom will warn me to never take that first puff of marijuana, because it leads to harder drugs. However, experience will also tell you, *after* you have wrestled with a cocaine and heroin addiction, that you never should have taken that first puff of marijuana. The problem with experience is that it's always hindsight. Wisdom is always foresight. Once you experience something, it's too late, because you have already done it. Wisdom will keep you from doing it in the first place! That's why wisdom is the best teacher, not experience. If you can learn from someone else's wisdom, you can avoid a lot of unnecessary bad experiences.

One of the greatest nuggets of wisdom concerning yokes of bondage is found in 2 Corinthians, where the Apostle Paul writes:

> Be ye not unequally yoked together with unbelievers: for what fellowship hath righteousness with unrighteousness? and what communion hath light with darkness? And what concord hath Christ with Belial? or what part hath he that believeth with an infidel? And what agreement hath the temple of God with idols? for ye are the temple of the living God; as God hath said, I will dwell in them, and walk in *them*; and I will be their God, and they shall be my people. Wherefore come out from among them, and be ye separate, saith the Lord, and touch not the unclean *thing*; and I will receive you.
> 2 Corinthians 6:14-17

One of the greatest things about wisdom is that it is not rocket science. The above passage is an example of the simplicity that is in the Gospel. This scripture clearly warns us not to become unequally yoked (tied together, united) with someone who is not a believer. In other words, a believer should never marry an unbeliever. I don't care how much attraction or what kind of chemistry there is between you. In most cases, those who fail to heed this simple wisdom run into some very complicated problems. More often than not, when a believer weds a non-believer, any spirits that the non-believer has can transfer and begin to negatively affect the believer. However, this type of transference will not work in reverse. In other words, just because the believer has the Holy Spirit, when the believer comes together intimately with the unbeliever, the Holy Ghost will not transfer to the unbeliever's spirit.

When a non-believer has intimate relations with a believer, the stronghold spirit only needs the lust of the flesh to find agreement. Both the believer and the non-believer have a fleshly sinful nature that serves as a basis to make a connection. In this case, the believer is compromised, not the unbeliever. Demonic spirits are transferable; the Holy Spirit is not. this is because the Holy Spirit can only be received by faith, and by having accepted Jesus as Lord and Savior, which involves hearing and believing the Gospel and repenting from sin.

A graphic illustration of how illicit sexual contact can have grave spiritual consequences can be seen in the account of King Solomon's idolatry. The word of God reads:

> But king Solomon loved many strange women, together with the daughter of Pharaoh, women

of the Moabites, Ammonites, Edomites, Zidonians, *and* Hittites; Of the nations *concerning* which the LORD said unto the children of Israel, Ye shall not go in to them, neither shall they come in unto you: *for* surely they will turn away your heart after their gods: Solomon clave unto these in love. And he had seven hundred wives, princesses, and three hundred concubines: and his wives turned away his heart. For it came to pass, when Solomon was old, *that* his wives turned away his heart after other gods: and his heart was not perfect with the LORD his God, as *was* the heart of David his father. For Solomon went after Ashtoreth the goddess of the Zidonians, and after Milcom the abomination of the Ammonites. And Solomon did evil in the sight of the LORD, and went not fully after the LORD, as *did* David his father. Then did Solomon build an high place for Chemosh, the abomination of Moab, in the hill that *is* before Jerusalem, and for Molech, the abomination of the children of Ammon. And likewise did he for all his strange wives, which burnt incense and sacrificed unto their gods.

1 Kings 11:1-8

Here we see that King Solomon's weakness for strange flesh became the conduit in which the enemy exploited him. The enemy set up soul-ties through sexual activity that caused Solomon to worship the idol gods of his numerous partners. Israel had been warned, "Ye shall not go in to them, neither shall they come in unto you: *for* surely they will turn away your heart after their gods." The New Living Translation says, "You must not marry them, because they will turn your hearts to their gods." The Lord knew that through sexual activity sanctioned by marriage, the spirits of those who worshipped the idols would be transferred to God's people and they would, in turn, turn away from God and start worshipping idols. Listen to what the bible says about those who worship idols:

> What say I then? that the idol is any thing, or that which is offered in sacrifice to idols is any thing? But I say, that the things which the Gentiles sacrifice, they sacrifice to Devils, and not to God: and I would not that ye should have fellowship with Devils. Ye cannot drink the cup of the Lord, and the cup of Devils: ye cannot be partakers of the Lord's table, and of the table of Devils.
> 1 Corinthians 10:19-21

People who worship idols are actually worshiping the demons behind them. So if a believer starts having sex with a person who worships idols, the demonic spirit operating behind that person will soul-tie transfer to the other person. That soul-tie transfer will have such a profound effect on the other person, that they will forsake God and start worshipping the idols attached to that demon. This is what caused King Solomon to turn from God. And this is why God warned Israel not to intermarry with idol worshipers.

The good news is that no matter what type of stronghold spirit attempts to keep you in bondage, Isaiah 10:27 encourages us because it says, "And it shall come to pass in that day, that his burden shall be taken away from off thy shoulder, and his yoke from off thy neck, and the yoke shall be destroyed because of the anointing."

Chapter 9

Receive Your Deliverance!

Now that we have completed an in-depth study of the many aspects of how evil spirits can adversely affect our lives, you may be feeling a little overwhelmed. However, there is a silver lining behind this black cloud. I say to you today that you can be delivered. Understand first and foremost that demonic spirits are real. Spirits are nothing to play with. If you have a spirit that is on you from birth, or if it developed through your childhood or your adult life, no matter when it happened, you can be delivered. However, before deliverance can occur, you have to want to be delivered.

Unfortunately, this is where deliverance stops for many individuals, because they have grown accustomed to the torment and the abuse. Through the soul-tie, the stronghold spirit has become so intertwined within their own personality that they cannot see themselves as ever being free. The next thing that must be done is you must be willing to expose the spirit. If you want to be delivered, you can never cover it up. There is nothing that is so bad that you can't talk to someone about it, because you are not the only one who has ever gone through it. The Devil wants you to keep it secret to make you feel you are all alone, when you are not.

Seven Steps to Freedom

In order to help you get on the right road to deliverance, I have found that there are some necessary steps that must be taken. Below I have listed the "Seven Steps to Deliverance." Each step will get you closer to your deliverance. In order to keep you on the path to freedom, each step is fortified with an accompanying passage of scripture.

Step one:
Admittance / Acknowledgement
(of your faults)

You must understand that until you first admit and acknowledge that you have a problem, you will never get delivered. The Devil wants you to be in fear of him and he keeps you in fear by holding secrets inside. He keeps you afraid to expose him. He will suggest that people are going to laugh at you and talk about you behind your back. But remember, you have the power to take control over the Devil and that destructive spirit by telling the truth. It is the light of the truth that makes you free. So admittance and acknowledging are the first powerful weapons in your arsenal to fight and be victorious over the Devil and his angels.

> Have mercy upon me, O God, according to thy loving kindness; according unto the multitude of thy tender mercies blot out my transgressions. Wash me thoroughly from mine iniquity, and cleanse me from my sin. For I acknowledge my transgressions; and my sin is ever before me.
> Psalm 51:1-3

Step two:
Ask God's Forgiveness and Forgive Others

Forgiveness is a very powerful weapon in our arsenal. However, there are two sides to this coin, which are *forgiveness* and *unforgiveness*. One is of God, the other is of the Devil. Understanding the necessity to operate in forgiveness, the Apostle Paul writes:

> To whom ye forgive any thing, I forgive also: for if I forgave any thing, to whom I forgave it, for your sakes forgave I it in the person of Christ; Lest Satan should get an advantage of us: for we are not ignorant of his devices.
> 2 Corinthians 2:10-11

As Paul clearly says, "For your sakes forgave I it in the person of Christ; Lest Satan should get an advantage of us." When we do not forgive, we open the door for the Devil to take advantage of us. Unforgiveness is one of the Devil's powerful devices that he uses against us. Therefore, it is absolutely necessary that we have forgiving hearts.

Forgiveness is a burden releaser. It is very difficult to continue carrying the weight of hate on your shoulders. Many times, people hurt others because they themselves are in pain. Sometimes the Devil can make us feel so terrible about ourselves, we feel that we cannot be forgiven. When we feel that there is no forgiveness for us, we won't ask to be forgiven. As long as the Devil can weigh us down with the burdens of unforgiveness, he can keep us in bondage. We will be just like the elephant that cannot break the flimsy chain that binds him.

We always need to understand that a necessary aspect of God's being is his love. And in his love is forgiveness and mercy. God is a forgiving God because He is a loving God. However, you have to want to be forgiven. Once you have asked God to forgive you, you must have the faith to know that He has forgiven you. Once He has forgiven you, you also have the courage to forgive yourself. When you can forgive yourself, you will then be able to forgive others around you.

> In whom we have redemption through his blood, the forgiveness of sins.
> Colossians 1:14

> ...For I will forgive their iniquity, and I will remember their sin no more.
> Jeremiah 31:34

> And when ye stand praying forgive, if ye have aught against any: that your father also which is in heaven may forgive you your trespasses.

But if ye do not forgive, neither will your father which is in heaven forgive your trespasses.
Mark 11:25-26

... Visiting the iniquities of the fathers upon the children unto the third and fourth generation of them that hate me; and showing mercy unto thousands of them that love me and keep my commandments.
Exodus 20:5-6

God will have mercy on you and forgive you when you keep his commandments.

Step Three:
Repent to God / Repent to Others

I tell you, nay: but, except ye repent, ye shall all likewise perish.
Luke 13:3

Repent ye therefore, and be converted that your sins may be blotted out for when the time of refreshing shall come, from the presence of the Lord.
Acts 3:19

Repenting to God and telling him that you are sorry for all that you have done is not hard to do. The reason I say that it's not hard to do is because God created you, and He knows everything about you. He also knows every thought before you think it. Even though He knows all about you, He still wants to hear it from your mouth and from your heart. Repenting is an open confession of your sins. In Matthew 3:8, John the Baptist tells the Pharisees, "Bring forth therefore fruits meet for repentance." The term "meet for repentance" means that you must be sincere when you are repenting to God. You have to have godly sorrow and contrition or remorse for your sins, as David had, for David prayed to the Lord and said:

> Against thee, thee only have I sinned and done this evil in thy sight that thou mightiest be justified when thou speakest, and clear when thou judgest.... The sacrifices of God are a broken spirit: a broken and a contrite heart, O God, thou wilt not despise.
> Psalms 51:4, 17

Another important aspect to repentance involves repentance to others, which is not as easy as repenting to God. We can't see God. We can pray to him in private and no one else knows. But we can't do that with people. We have to face them, especially the ones you may have hurt. Repenting to people involves a lot of humility and swallowing of pride, both of which can be very difficult to do.

The enemy will keep an unrepentant spirit in your heart to keep the stronghold spirit connected to you. The enemy will have you always blaming someone else and making excuses for why you committed the wrong you perpetrated on others. You have to (as I did) pray and ask God for strength to go to that individual and ask, "Will you forgive me for the way I've felt towards you?" Though it may seem like this is a position of weakness, it actually is a moment of empowerment.

Unfortunately, many saved persons find it hard to ask someone for forgiveness, but that is nothing but pride working. Failing to go to someone that you have offended will stifle your relationship with the Lord. In Matthew 5:24, Jesus tells us, "Leave there thy gift before the alter, and go thy way; first be reconciled to thy brother, and then come and offer thy gift." In this generation, we put so much emphasis on gifting, that we forget from whom we receive our gifts. Your gifting will mean nothing if you will not reconcile with those who have aught against you.

There are also times that you will have to go to an individual and say to them, "I forgive you for the things you've done to me." Yes, sometimes you will have to initiate the healing process yourself. Release them. Tell them that you forgive them. Many people are walking around bound with other people's sins perpetrated upon them in the past. There are people who were molested as children still carrying the burdens of guilt and low self-esteem. There are numerous cases of children in foster homes who were physically abused in terrible ways, and the deep emotional wounds have never healed years later.

Just like physical scars, emotional scars never go away. Years ago, there was a young man who wanted me to pray with him for deliverance. During prayer one day, the Spirit prompted me to tell him to "forgive them." I asked him who "them" was. He stated that at one time he and his brother were foster children. The foster parents treated them like slave labor, having them cleaning all day long. If their foster parents felt their chores were not completed right, they would be beaten, and then tied up and left in a closet without eating. They also had to endure being burned with cigarette butts. I told him that in order for him to receive a complete deliverance, he needed to forgive them.

This young man told me he would never forgive them! No, never! He said, "I can't believe God would have me forgive them." This young man was so bitter that he refused to pray any longer. The wounds and scars were so deep that he was unable to forgive the foster parents for what they had done to him and his brother years earlier. This young man was under the stronghold of drugs and alcohol. He never received his deliverance, and died from an overdose of drugs. Unfortunately, he thought that forgiving them was the same thing as excusing them, but it is not. Forgiving them doesn't excuse them because they still have to give an account to God, who will judge them himself. Forgiving them would have released him, so he would not have had to keep carrying that heavy burden that eventually destroyed him. Unfortunately, because of unforgiveness, Satan was able to get the advantage. Remember, forgiveness is a two-sided coin – heads is freedom, tails is bondage. If you want complete deliverance, you will do whatever it takes to be free.

Step Four:
Resist the Devil /Stop the Behavior /Stay Away!

During the Regan Administration, First Lady Nancy Regan headed up an anti-drug campaign where they coined the phrase, "Just Say No." However, little did many know at the time that simply saying no is powerless when it comes to fighting spiritual wickedness in high places. It is true that we must take a stand against the Devil, however, it requires a lot more than just saying no. The bible says, "Submit yourselves therefore to God. Resist the Devil, and he will flee from you" (James 4:7).

In order to effectively resist the Devil from drawing you back to those destructive behaviors, you will need Holy Ghost power and God's Words. The Devil doesn't mind you "just saying no" if that's all the resistance from you that he's going to get. He already knows that those words could never stop him. While he has you bound up, you could still be "just saying no."

It is very important that we use wisdom to avoid certain persons, places and things, if we are going to maintain our freedom and deliverance. In Amos 3:3, the scripture asks us a very important question: can two walk together except they be agreed? After you are delivered, you must avoid former friends who can't understand your new life in Christ Jesus. They are still in darkness and live by the dictates of "the prince of the power of the air" – the Devil. You are now a child of God who walks in the light of the Lord. What fellowship does light have with darkness?

One day a little boy hopped a neighbor's fence to get his ball. After jumping into the neighbor's yard, the boy was bitten on his rear by the neighbor's dog. When the boy went crying to his mother about being bitten, to his surprise his mother didn't cuddle him and say, "Aw, poor little baby." She said, "Let this be a lesson to you. You had no business in that yard." There are consequences for hopping over in the Devil's yard. However, in the Devil's backyard there won't be any Cocker Spaniels; there will be a roaring lion waiting to see who he can devour.

Deliverance

Therefore, stay away from toxic places and change your friends. The old saying "birds of a feather flock together" is true. You will have to get some new friends. You want to surround yourself with people of the same mind. I tried to continue having friends who were fornicators and adulterers. I thought I was strong enough to handle their contrary lifestyle. But I quickly learned that I had to leave them alone, because continuing those associations would only lead to me returning to stronghold bondage once again. You must run for your life! There is also another saying, that you are known by the company you keep.

As it states in 2 Corinthians 6:17-18,

> Wherefore come out from among them, and be ye separated, saith the Lord, and touch not the unclean thing; and I will receive you, and will be a father unto you, and ye shall be my sons and daughters, saith the Lord Almighty.

You must come away from all things that are not clean. Separate yourself from girlfriends, boyfriends, smoking, drinking, drugs, evil, etc. Stay away from these things. Don't touch these things. Don't handle these things. If you continue to stay around these things and people, you will be right back into it, and then you will end up in worse condition than you were in the first place. In John 5:14, after the Lord heals the lame man, the bible says: "Afterward Jesus findeth him in the temple, and said unto him, Behold, thou art made whole: sin no more, lest a worse thing come unto thee." This lets us know that the condition that this man suffered from was the result of an immoral lifestyle. Therefore Jesus warns him to "sin no more" or a worse condition will come upon him.

First of all, no matter how bad we think we had it, it can always be worse. Secondly, we need to stop making occasion for the flesh. If you plan to sin, you will sin. No matter what you might say, there is no good reason to call up an old fling. Romans 13:14 says, "But put ye on the Lord Jesus Christ, and make not provision for the flesh, to fulfill the lusts thereof." If you intentionally go against God's warning, then Peter tells us what we have to look forward to.

> For if after they have escaped the pollutions of the world through the knowledge of the Lord and Saviour Jesus Christ, they are again entangled therein, and overcome, the latter end is worse with them than the beginning. For it had been better for them not to have known the way of righteousness, than, after they have known *it*, to turn from the holy commandment delivered unto them. But it is happened unto them according to the true proverb, The dog *is* turned to his own vomit again; and the sow that was washed to her wallowing in the mire.
> 2 Peter 2:20-22

Step Five:
Sanctify Yourself / Get Into the Truth

An important thing that must be done in order to maintain your deliverance is you must purge yourself of any representations of the strongholds that kept you bound. In the book of Acts, we get a graphic account of Sceva and his sons, who foolishly attempted to exorcise a demon without any Holy Ghost power. The demon came out of the possessed man and then leaped on them. However, it is what follows that event that I would like to emphasize here. The passage reads:

> And the man in whom the evil spirit was leaped on them, and overcame them, and prevailed against them, so that they fled out of that house naked and wounded. And this was known to all the Jews and Greeks also dwelling at Ephesus; and fear fell on them all, and the name of the Lord Jesus was magnified. And many that believed came, and confessed, and shewed their deeds. Many of them also which used curious arts brought their books together, and burned them before all *men*: and they counted the price of them, and found *it* fifty thousand *pieces* of silver.
> Acts 19:16-19

They collected their books on curious arts (the occult) and burned them. This scripture tells us that you must purge yourself of the remembrances of sin.

As we have already covered, the remembrance of these things war against your soul. Therefore, you must rid yourself of books, tapes, clothes, DVD's, phone numbers, Face book accounts, My Space, Twitter, delete certain telephone numbers out of your phone book, etc. Getting rid of the things and cleansing you of reminders and other triggers that can lead you back into those wicked behaviors will help you stay free of strongholds. If you do not smoke any more, throw away any remaining cigarettes and ashtrays. Do not buy them, do not carry them, and do not hold them. Do not hang around people who are smoking, and do not allow smoking in your house.

Whatever your stronghold was, completely eliminate ways to go back into those things. As Isaiah admonished his people, "Wash you, make you clean; put away the evil of your doings from before mine eyes; cease to do evil; Learn to do well..." (Isaiah 1:16-17).

Step six:
Receive the Holy Ghost / Get the Power!

In 2 Corinthians 5:17, we find out about one of the greatest power-packed dynamics of the Spirit filled life. This familiar passage says, "Therefore if any man *be* in Christ, *he is* a new creature: old things are passed away; behold, all things are become new." In this passage of scripture, you have the words "new creature," which actually means "new creation." As Christians, once we are born again in the Spirit, we are totally new. The old things, such as the old sinful behaviors and the strongholds that had us bound, are the "old things that have passed away." However, this is a positional and spiritual reality. Down here where the rubber meets the road, we still have to struggle with our own weakness and the attacks of the enemy. Therefore, we need power to stand our ground in holiness and righteousness. In order to do that, we need the Holy Spirit. In Acts 1:8, we find these powerful words, "But ye shall receive power after that the Holy Ghost is come upon you: and ye shall be witnesses unto me both in Jerusalem, and Samaria, and unto the uttermost part of the earth." In step 4, we discussed the issue of just saying no to the Devil. Since the Devil is a spirit, mere human words have no power to restrain him. However, with the Holy Spirit, God gives us the power to be more than conquerors and the power to be effective witnesses.

The witnessing of the Holy Spirit working through us is more than the world against us. When Jesus was on the earth, He was the comforter for his Disciples. He knew He had to leave them, and they would be without the power to resist the Devil; therefore He told the Disciples where to go to get the Power. It is this power that every one of us needs to resist the power of the Devil's temptations. Understand that it's not enough to just go to church and hear the word of God, and not receive the power of God. There are many who go to church and commit sinful acts all the time because they don't have the power. The Bible tells us of these people, "Having a form of godliness but denying the power thereof." (2 Timothy 3:5) However, if you are truly born again, you are also a new creation in Christ where old things have passed away, and all thing are become new!

Step Seven:
Pray and Fast Always

In order to be successful in your deliverance, you must be able to maintain a constant prayer and fasting life. In I Thessalonians 5:17, it tells us to pray without ceasing. When you are asking God for the deliverance of a stronghold, you cannot let up in your prayer. The Devil is waiting for the time when you are weak, so he can enter back into your life. We have to constantly stay prayed up! The enemy is always waiting to exploit any weaknesses you have in the flesh through temptation. Jesus told his disciples in Mark 14:38, "Watch ye and pray, lest ye enter into temptation; the spirit is indeed willing but the flesh is weak." If the Devil is bold enough to tempt Jesus, the Son of God, he will definitely tempt you. And Jesus also told His disciples in Mark 9:28-29, that certain spirits will only come out with both prayer and fasting.

In Luke 22:31. Jesus gives Peter an astonishing revelation concerning what the Devil wanted to do to him. The passage tells us, "And the Lord said, Simon, Simon, behold, Satan hath desired to have you, that he may sift you as wheat." Jesus is letting Peter know that Satan has taken a certain interest in having his way with him. However, in verse 32, Jesus tells Peter, "But I have prayed for thee, that thy faith fail not." Jesus' remedy for warding off Satan's attack on Peter was that He *prayed* for Peter. It is interesting that Jesus didn't say that He prayed that the Father would send warring angels to set a hedge about Peter, or that He would hide Peter in his secret place, or some other deep thing. But Jesus said that He prayed that Peter's faith failed not.

From this, we can see that there is a direct connection between prayer, faith and getting the victory over the Devil. In 1 John 5:4, the bible tells us: "For whatsoever is born of God overcometh the world: and this is the victory that overcometh the world, even our faith." In Ephesians 6:18, the bible says: "Praying always with all prayer and supplication in the Spirit." Then in Jude 20, were are told how we must build up our most holy faith. The Word of God says:

> But ye, beloved, building up yourselves on your most holy faith, praying in the Holy Ghost.

The text is clear here: we build up our faith by praying in the Holy Ghost. This is why Jesus prayed that Peter's faith failed not, because it's faith that overcomes the world and prevents Satan from having his way with us. But we won't have the power behind our faith if we do not pray. In the above passage, the words "building up" our faith basically means "to restore by building." When we pray, our faith and Christian walk become more solid and consistent. This is why prayer is so important to maintaining our deliverance and freedom from strongholds. Know prayer, know victory. No prayer, no victory.

The question then becomes "how do we pray and what do we pray?" Jesus tells us in Matthew 6:9-13, "After this manner therefore pray ye: Our Father which art in heaven, Hallowed be thy name. Thy kingdom come. Thy will be done in earth, as it is in heaven. Give us this day our daily bread. And forgive us our debts, as we forgive our debtors. And lead us not into temptation, but deliver us from evil: For thine is the kingdom, and the power, and the glory, for ever Amen."

Chapter 10

Final Exhortations

After having many years of personal experience dealing with strongholds, this book was written on behalf of all the people who are suffering from demonic oppression as well. I did not write this book to glorify sin or wickedness, neither did I want to give the impression that I am better than anyone else. But because this is such a prevalent and important issue, the silence had to be broken. Demonic spirits are real and they need to be treated seriously.

There are many spirits that could be on you from birth, and there are also spirits that come upon you at different stages of your life. However, sin is the doorway to the demonic. People who walk in righteousness have a far less chance of the enemy invading their lives. Whenever someone traffics in evil, that is the key that unlocks the door to evil spirits. The scripture tell us, "...visiting the iniquity of the fathers unto the third and fourth generation of them that hate me" (Exodus 20:5). The iniquity of the father is their sin that they committed against God. God will put conditions upon or allow spirits from the Devil to come upon the children of those men and women who sin willfully against God. "For if we sin willfully after that we have received the knowledge of the truth, there remaineth no more sacrifice for sins" (Hebrews 10:26).

This is why I believe many children are born with special needs issues or birth defects. Now I know that this may sound unbelievable, and some may feel that I am being overly critical or even paranoid about demonic activity. However, let me back this statement up with what the bible has to say about demons and children. In Matthew 17, the scripture gives an account of distressed father looking for deliverance for his son. The passage says:

> Lord, have mercy on my son: for he is lunatick, and sore vexed: for ofttimes he falleth into the fire, and oft into the water. And I brought him to thy disciples, and they could not cure him. Then Jesus answered and said, O faithless and perverse generation, how long shall I be with you? how long shall I suffer you? bring him hither to me. And Jesus rebuked the Devil; and he departed out of him: and the child was cured from that very hour. Then came the disciples to Jesus apart, and said, Why could not we cast him out? And Jesus said unto them, Because of your unbelief: for verily I say unto you, If ye have faith as a grain of mustard seed, ye shall say unto this mountain, Remove hence to yonder place; and it shall remove; and nothing shall be

impossible unto you. Howbeit this kind goeth not out but by prayer and fasting.
>
> Matthew 17:15-21

In this passage, the word lunatick (or lunatic) is used in the King James Version. However, in the Amplified Version, the word is "epilepsy," which is a debilitating seizure disorder. This same disorder that we see today is treated with medication, but as the bible tells us, the cause of this little boy's epilepsy was demonic. I have heard many people; men and women, boys and girls, say, "I don't know what causes me to behave the way that I do."

Without God's intervention, these stronghold spirits are uncontrollable. Even though people may want to stop, they cannot on their own. For example, there are men and women who look at pornography knowing that it's wrong, and they want to stop but their will power fails them. There are men and women who are sexually promiscuous and want to stop but cannot. There are also people who hate people or have spirits of jealously, envy or prejudice, who don't want to be that way, but they cannot change themselves.

There are some people who will read this book and say, "He should be ashamed of himself." Or they may also feel "he should not be telling all his business." However, I don't feel ashamed – I feel liberated! In the Amplified Bible, James 5:16 says:

> Confess to one another therefore your faults (your slips, your false steps, your offenses, your sins) and pray [also] for one another, that you may be healed and restored [to a spiritual tone

of mind and heart]. The earnest (heartfelt, continued) prayer of a righteous man makes tremendous power available [dynamic in its working].

As I wrote in the previous chapter, the first step to your deliverance is to acknowledge that you have a spirit on you, because the bible also says, "....for the accuser of our brethren is cast down, which accused them before our God day and night. And they overcame him by the blood of the Lamb, and by the word of their testimony..." (Revelation 12:10-11) When we confess our sins, and we follow-up with our testimony of deliverance, that's how you cast down and defeat the Devil!

The Enemy Wants You To Hide Your Sins

Stop hiding it! Stop being ashamed of it! Do not go to your grave with this secret. There are two reasons why you should tell it before you go to your grave with it. First, because you want your deliverance, to assure that you've made it into heaven. Secondly, you want to deliver your message to help somebody else. If you have children or grandchildren, they need to know, the world needs to know that they can have a spirit on them but be delivered.

To write your story and tell the truth is cathartic and very liberating. In John 8:36, it states, "If the Son shall therefore make you free ye are free indeed." For a long time, I wanted to write this book because I'm no longer afraid of the Devil. Now I know that he can't do anything to me anymore.

The enemy would attempt to torment me by telling me that my past was going to eventually catch up with me. He would then insist that my ministerial career would be in ruins if the wrong individuals found out the truth about my past. Well today, I don't have anything to hide and certainly nothing to be embarrassed about. I'm not worried about my career or my title, or my position in the community being damaged, because I'm free.

With a vengeance, I would preach messages against the kingdom of darkness that deal with demons and stronghold spirits. What the Devil meant for my harm, God turned it around for my good, and the good of others who will learn from my experiences, and find deliverance too.

The Enemy Will Continue To Come At You

The enemy is not convinced that you are no longer going to be bound by him. He will stop at nothing to overtake you once again. The enemy will start pursuing you and bringing more temptations at you than ever before. However, 1 Corinthians 10:13 assures us that:

> There hath no temptation taken you but such as is common to man: but God *is* faithful, who will not suffer you to be tempted above that ye are able; but will with the temptation also make a way to escape, that ye may be able to bear *it.*

Yes, the enemy will continue to search for weaknesses in your defenses to try to regain control. I remember after the Lord delivered me that I was in the grocery store and there was a woman I said hello to. What did I do that for? This started a conversation with her that I didn't really want. However, once I opened that door, she started telling me all about her life and what she was going through. In my mind, I was simply being "nice," but I ended up receiving unsolicited conversation and attention. Then this woman started following me throughout the store. Every aisle I went down, there she was coming up the other end trying to continue the conversation. She came down another aisle, and out of nowhere had the temerity to say, "I haven't been with a man in six months." Somewhat shocked, I told her I wasn't interested. However, she was persistent and caught up with me right before I entered the checkout line and said, "I only live a few minutes away from here." I didn't even acknowledge her because I knew it was really the enemy behind it all.

The Devil will continue to pursue you in hopes that you will succumb to his enticements. However, I did not give in because to give in is also to give up. I held on to my integrity and stayed saved. This is the reason why it is important to be strong in the Lord. You will need the power of the Holy Ghost. You cannot successfully resist the Devil on your own power. Therefore, be wise and strong in the Lord and the power of his might. Keep your spiritual guns loaded up with Holy Ghost power!

Everyone Needs Deliverance!

When it comes to deliverance, people tend to focus on the big things like sex or drugs. However, the Devil has a long list of strongholds. Remember it's "the little foxes that spoil

the vines." (Song of Solomon 2:15) The truth is, everybody has something that is working in them that they need to be delivered from, whether they know it or not. In
I John 1:8-10, the bible states,

> If we say that we have no sin, we deceive ourselves, and the truth is not in us. If we confess our sins, he is faithful and just to forgive us *our* sins, and to cleanse us from all unrighteousness. If we say that we have not sinned, we make him a liar, and his word is not in us.

This is not justification to sin; this is again acknowledgement that we were intrinsically sinful. Can one then say, since I was born this way, and I have God's grace, and He will forgive me, why worry about sin? Apostle Paul would beg to differ with that and make this argument: "What shall we say then? Shall we continue in sin, that grace may abound? God forbid. How shall we that are dead to sin live any longer therein?" (Romans 6:1-2)

Don't try to hide it because the bible says; "...behold, ye have sinned against the LORD: and be sure your sin will find you out" (Numbers 32:23). Besides, the longer you hide it, you give the Devil more power to maintain control over you. Remember, the Devil is not your friend. He only comes to kill, steal and destroy you.

In order to find and keep your deliverance, you must hunger and thirst after it. As David states in Psalm 42:1, "As the hart panteth after the water brooks, so panteth my soul after thee, O God." I don't care how long you have been struggling, or how long you have been trying to cope with it, it has only been eating you up inside for years. Even though you have excelled and have reached great heights in your status in life and achieved success in your career, this stronghold will not go away. If you do not destroy it at the root, like a weed, it will always come back. And like cockroaches on the wall, this spirit may come out when you least expect it to.

One might ask, why is the Devil so bent on destroying us? Number one, we are made in the image of God, and God loved us so much that when we fell, He put a plan of salvation into action to save us – something that He didn't do for the Devil and his angels. And secondly, we are kings, queens and royal priest. We are also God's sons and daughters and joint-heirs with Christ, with an eternal inheritance laid up for us in heaven, that's kept by the power of God. This is why the enemy is so upset with all of us. He wants to completely destroy you to get back at God. However, he will never win in the end because he can never thwart God's plans.

So finally, my brothers and sisters let me say that whatever spirit confronts you, whatever spirit you wrestle with, whatever curses that may have been placed upon your life, you can be delivered. There is nothing too hard for God. I AM SAVED! I AM DELIVERED! I AM FREE! However; just because I am delivered, I don't stop praying, fasting, and keeping my mind stayed on Jesus. "Thou wilt keep him in perfect peace, whose mind is stayed on thee: because he trusteth in thee" (Isaiah 26:3). God has good things in store for those who walk upright. The Word says, "For the LORD God is a sun and shield: the LORD will give grace and glory: no good thing will he withhold from them that walk uprightly" (Psalm 84:11). You are not doomed! There is hope for you through the word of your testimony and the blood of the Lamb.

The End

Deliverance

Life To Legacy

Let us bring your story to life! With Life to Legacy, we offer the following publishing services: Manuscript development, editing and transcription services, cover design, copyright services, ISBN assignment and much more. You maintain control over your project because we are here to serve you.

Even if you do not have a manuscript, we can ghostwrite your story for you from audio recordings and even legible handwritten documents. We also specialize in family history books. Let us bring your legacy to literary life!

Please visit our website:
www.Life2legacy.com, or call us at 877-267-7477.
You can also email us @ Life2legacybooks@att.net

www.ingramcontent.com/pod-product-compliance
Lightning Source LLC
Chambersburg PA
CBHW070053120426
42742CB00048B/2506